Forty Years
1963-2003

Forty Years 1963-2003

Department of Sociology University of Toronto

EDITED BY RICK HELMES-HAYES
EDITORIAL ASSISTANCE PROVIDED BY ANNE MITCHELL

Canadian Scholars' Press Inc.
Toronto

Forty Years, 1963-2003, Department of Sociology, University of Toronto

Edited by Rick Helmes-Hayes
Editorial assistance provided by Anne Mitchell

First published in 2003 by
Canadian Scholars' Press Inc.
180 Bloor Street West, Suite 801
Toronto, Ontario M5S 2V6
www.cspi.org

CSPI gratefully acknowledges financial support for our publishing activities from the Government of Canada through the Book Publishing Industry Development Program (BPIDP) and the Government of Ontario through the Ontario Book Initiative.

National Library of Canada Cataloguing in Publication Data

Department of Sociology, University of Toronto : 40 years, 1963-2003 / edited by Rick Helmes-Hayes ; editorial assistance provided by Anne Mitchell.
ISBN 1-55130-228-4

1. University of Toronto. Dept. of Sociology—History. 2. Sociology—Study and teaching (Higher)—Ontario—Toronto. I. Helmes-Hayes, Richard C. (Richard Charles), 1951- II. Mitchell, Anne, 1969-

HM578.C3D46 2003 301'.071'1713541 C2003-904279-0

Cover design, text design and layout by Zack Taylor. The Department of Sociology logo was designed under the direction of Professor Dean Behrens.

03 04 05 06 07 08 7 6 5 4 3 2 1

Printed and bound in Canada by AGMV Marquis Imprimeur Inc.
Canadä

This volume is dedicated to the following tenured faculty members, sadly deceased:

Norman W. Bell
Howard Boughey
Jean-Louis de Lannoy
Lewis Feuer
Robert L. James
Rex A. Lucas
Peter K. New
Harry K. Nishio
Ian Weinberg

Table of Contents

List of Photographs

Preface

The mission statement of the Department of Sociology is "Excellence in Teaching and Research," and over the past forty years, this mission has been exceeded. The department is an extremely productive research and teaching enterprise. Faculty obtain a large number of research grants, awarded by the Social Science and Humanities Research Council and other funding organizations. Their publications include a record number of cutting-edge articles and books. The external reviewers for the Ontario Council of Graduate Studies in 2000 were very impressed by the strength and research diversity of the faculty, noting that they are "… held in high esteem in the international community of sociology."

Teaching and graduate supervision is a priority. The undergraduate program is one of the largest in the Faculty of Arts and Science. Seven faculty members have been awarded the prestigious Arts and Science Outstanding Teaching Award. A total of 244 graduate students completed their Ph.D. theses, and the majority pursued academic careers at Canadian, American, and European universities.

As noted in this volume, the department's forty-year journey has, at times, been tumultuous; however, the driving force has always been excellence in teaching and research.

Dennis William Magill
Professor, Department of Sociology
University of Toronto
June 9, 2003

Preface

Department of Sociology, University of Toronto: In Context

Department of Sociology, University of Toronto: In Context[1]

RICK HELMES-HAYES

Fifteen years have passed since the twenty-fifth anniversary volume appeared in 1988. In my "Editor's Introduction" to that book, I opened my remarks with the following statement:

> As its title may be a trifle deceiving, it should be noted at the outset that this little book does not provide a comprehensive, critical history of the University of Toronto Department of Sociology since 1963. That is not its purpose. Instead, it has been put together as a memento intended to celebrate the department's twenty-fifth anniversary.

In one sense, what I wrote fifteen years ago could simply be retyped, substituting "fortieth anniversary" for "twenty-fifth." Certainly, the celebratory purpose of the book is paramount. The University of Toronto Department of Sociology now has a forty-year history as arguably the "flagship" department in the country. However, to describe this book as a purely celebratory volume would be to underplay the historical significance of what is to be found in the following pages. This work makes available to historians of Canadian sociology materials that—to my knowledge—exist for no other department of sociology in the country, and provide a very sound underpinning to the writing of a comprehensive history of the department.

The contents of the 1988 work, *A Quarter-Century of Sociology at the University of Toronto, 1963-1988*, while substantial and interesting, are much less meaty than the contents of this book. The first contained essays by S.D. Clark and Oswald Hall, each an eminent pioneer of Canadian sociology, each a Fellow of the Royal Society of Canada. Clark's contributions to the discipline have been thoroughly documented and assessed in Deborah Harrison's *The Limits of Liberalism* (1981), Harry Hiller's *Society and*

Change (1982), and a series of essays collected in Dennis Magill and William Michelson's *Images of Change* (1999). For his part, Hall's career has been examined by David Nock (1987) and celebrated in a *Festschrift* edited by Audrey Wipper: *The Sociology of Work: Essays in Honour of Oswald Hall* (1984).

Clark's essay in *A Quarter-Century of Sociology at the University of Toronto* outlined the events that culminated in the establishment of sociology as a separate department in 1963. His is an essentially descriptive account that reflects Clark's training as a social historian—a sense of historical context, a keen eye for detail, and an awareness of the role that key individuals played in establishing an independent Department of Sociology at the University of Toronto. Hall's essay has more the flavour of a contribution to the sociology of knowledge or the sociology of sociology. It compares the founding of the Toronto department with the founding of its "rival" at McGill University in Montreal, established in 1925. Rather than focus exclusively on the details of the establishment of the two departments, however, Hall offers fascinating and insightful answers to a series of more general questions about the social conditions which caused/allowed the discipline of sociology to develop in two very different ways at two very different universities in two very different urban environments. These original essays remain key historical accounts of the early days of the discipline and have been used by many historians of Canadian sociology over the past fifteen years. In addition, the book also contained other useful "nuts and bolts" information about the history of the department; specifically, comprehensive, year-by-year listings of faculty who had taught in the department from 1934-1935 to 1987-1988, and listings of Ph.D. dissertations completed in the department between 1925 and 1988.

In this book, the essays by Clark and Hall have been reproduced and, thanks to Anne Mitchell and Jeannette Wright, the lists of full-time faculty members and completed Ph.D. dissertations have been brought up to date. In a novel and exciting addition, this book contains five new essays that tell the tale of the department as it grew and changed between 1969 and 2003. Four of these essays are by former chairs of the department: Jim Giffen (1969-1972), Irving Zeitlin (1972-1977), Lorna Marsden (1977-1979), and John Simpson (1985-1996). A fifth was written by the current chair, Lorne Tepperman (1997-2003).[2] Jeffrey Reitz, who held the chair between 1980 and 1985, declined to contribute an essay. As a result, the account of his chairship is a brief summary based on the department files.[3] The essays by Giffen, Zeitlin, Marsden, and Simpson, in combination with the Clark and

Hall essays, the tape-recorded interviews with the chairs of the department, and other materials in the departmental Archives, when supplemented by the materials in the S.D. Clark Papers, the Lorna Marsden Papers, and the Rex A. Lucas Papers in the Robarts Library, provide a wealth of materials about the Toronto department. I suspect that no other department of sociology in Canada has an equivalent set of resource materials. Soon, perhaps, someone will undertake to write a formal history of the department. Certainly, that would be an important and worthwhile contribution to the history of the discipline in Canada for likely no department was as influential during the twentieth century as the one at the University of Toronto.

The earliest beginnings of sociology in Canada are tied to the Protestant Social Gospel movement and the activities of muckraking journalists and labour activists of the late nineteenth and early twentieth centuries. However, it was not until the establishment of the Sociology department at McGill University by Carl Dawson, in 1925, that a more recognizably modern form of academic sociology emerged. While Dawson and his colleagues recorded several successes in their efforts to build sociology at McGill between 1925 and the early 1960s,[4] sociology was only poorly developed elsewhere in Canada. There was an Honours program in sociology at Toronto, but Clark was for many years the only full-time appointment in the discipline and there were only a handful of appointments scattered across Canada's other universities. For his part, Clark developed a sociological approach that reflected the impact of his training as a historian, in particular the views of his mentor, Harold Innis, the powerful chair of the Department of Political Economy at Toronto. Clark employed the frontier thesis, the staples thesis, and some elements of sociological functionalism to carry out a series of studies of political, social, economic, and religious change on Canada's various pioneer frontiers (e.g., 1942, 1948, 1959). During the 1940s and 1950s, he bravely (and wisely) defended a historical and "British" conception of the discipline against the more scientific and presentist model that dominated U.S. sociology.

I noted above that despite the best efforts of Dawson, Clark, and their colleagues scattered across the country, sociology remained a marginal discipline in Canadian academic culture until the early 1960s, the date at which Professor Clark's essay leaves off. In order to provide a background for the essays by Professors Giffen, Zeitlin, and the others that tell the balance of the story beginning in around 1970, I should outline a few highlights from the 1960s.

Highlights are easy to find, not only in relation to sociology at Toronto, but also concerning the Canadian discipline at large, and Canadian post-secondary education more generally. In one sense, Clark's account of the slow process by which sociology grew at Toronto could be generalized across Canada. As late as 1960-1961, there were only sixty-one sociologists teaching in Canadian universities (Hiller, 1982:23, Table 3). However, coincident with Clark taking the chair in the early 1960s, there was an explosion in the Canadian post-secondary education system, and sociology was able to tag along for the ride.

Four basic factors created the economic, social, and political preconditions necessary for the rapid growth of the Canadian university system: (1) the extended post-war economic boom created a new economy increasingly dependent on a highly educated work force; (2) a newly-developed faith in education as the key to social justice and economic progress created popular, governmental, and corporate support for higher education; (3) thanks to the economic boom and the adoption of Keynesian economic practices, federal and provincial governments had tax revenues available to fund the expansion of the system; and (4) the "baby boom" generation matured to university entrance age and demanded entry (see Axelrod, 1982; Owram, 1996).

The consequent growth in the system was rapid, massive, and unprecedented. Between 1963-1964 and 1971-1972, undergraduate enrolment at Canadian universities doubled, from 141,000 to 287,000 (Dominion Bureau of Statistics, 1964:344, Table 8; see also Leacy et al., 1975:Series W340-438). Graduate enrolment quadrupled from 8,400 to 36,000 (Ibid.). Sociologists wisely took advantage of the opportunities provided by the funding bonanza and the intellectual and administrative openness of the era to expand the discipline and establish it firmly as a part of the new university curriculum. This was possible because of a new legitimacy the discipline enjoyed, fostered in part by the impact of John Porter's *The Vertical Mosaic*, published in 1965. In any case, by 1970, there were 829 sociologists teaching in Canadian universities, a fourteen-fold increase over the decade (Hiller, 1982:23, Table 3). This pattern was also seen in the Toronto department. Where in 1960-1961, the department had only six full-time faculty members, by 1971-1972 it had forty-four (Helmes-Hayes, 1988:61, 25-29).

There were other key developments in the discipline, as well. Sociologists and anthropologists broke away from the Canadian Political Science Association to form the Canadian Sociology and Anthropology Association in 1965 and, as part of the same process, founded their own journal, the

Canadian Review of Sociology and Anthropology (Jones, 1990). However, the rapid growth that created these and other opportunities (e.g., the increased availability of government research funding) also created some serious problems. Chief among them was that Canadian sociology departments had to hire large numbers of foreign nationals, in particular Americans, because Canadian graduate programs were woefully underdeveloped. This led to a situation where the sociology being taught in Canadian universities was largely U.S.-oriented. American professors taught American theories about American society using American texts. By 1970, there was widespread dissatisfaction with this U.S. domination of the discipline, and a nationalistic "Canadianization" movement developed in protest (see Hiller, 1979; Cormier, 2002). As Zeitlin's account of his chairship makes clear, the politics—academic and otherwise—of this situation created consequential and long-lasting problems at the University of Toronto.

Giffen and Zeitlin note that the Canadianization movement was not the only salient political force in the department in the late 1960s and early 1970s. Many of the faculty members hired by Clark during the 1960s came from an academic culture that was more democratic than Clark was willing to accommodate. In a fashion consistent with University regulations and the Toronto academic culture of the time, he ran the department as an old-style "Head." He consulted with an inner circle of senior colleagues, but had final say on all matters of hiring, policy, and the like, and was responsible only to the Dean of Arts and Science for his decisions. In a development echoed by other North American universities, newly hired faculty members (and some of what Zeitlin refers to as "the old guard"), many of them influenced by the civil rights movement, the anti-Vietnam War movement, the student movement, and so forth, demanded a bigger say in departmental governance. Clark balked and was subsequently "deposed" (to use Zeitlin's term) from the Chair.

Adding to the unrest created by the Canadianization issue and the governance issue was the appearance of Marxism and feminism. Both were, at one and the same time, scholarly and activism-oriented political perspectives. A number of creative, non-Stalinist Marxisms emerged in Europe, in particular the so-called "critical theory" of the Frankfurt School, and the Marxism of scholars such as E.P. Thompson (*The Making of the English Working Class*, 1963), Ralph Miliband (*The State in Capitalist Society*, 1969), and Harry Braverman (*Labor and Monopoly Capital*, 1974). These views became respectable in Canadian academia, including at the University of Toronto, which brought in the well-known Marx scholar, Lewis Feuer.

In Canada, as in Europe, these new "critical" sociologies were often loosely coupled with approaches such as ethnomethodology or phenomenology. A development unique to Canada was the mixture of this imported classical Marxism with the domestic liberal political economy of scholars such as Harold Innis; the domestic Marxist political economy of, for example, H. Clare Pentland (1981); the "Marxist" political philosophy of C.B. Macpherson (1965, 1973, 1978); and literature on Third World development and underdevelopment. This "made in Canada" approach, which came to be known as the "new political economy," helped to provide a fundamental theoretical, methodological, and practical-political critique of the "mainstream" (read "liberal") scientific and functionalist sociology of the time.[5] Indeed, as Zeitlin, Marsden, and others point out, these newly respectable critical sociologies touched off a set of highly divisive scholarly-political battles that influenced not just the U of T department, but departments across the country. This was the case in many other social science and humanities disciplines.

At the same time that the new political economy was beginning to make its presence felt, feminist scholarship emerged as a formidable scholarly and political force. Developed in a symbiotic relationship with the feminist movement, and buoyed by the *Report of the Royal Commission on the Status of Women*, feminist scholarship successfully challenged both mainstream and radical sociologists, including the "new political economists," to rethink their "malestream" political and scholarly assumptions and practices. The feminists' goal, then as now, was to contribute to the development of an inclusive, non-sexist sociology and society (see, e.g., Eichler, 2002).

It was against this backdrop that Professor Jim Giffen assumed the extremely sensitive and difficult role of Chair. For over two years, he presided over a situation remembered by many people as stressful and difficult. As his somewhat puckish and acerbic comments indicate, departmental politics became for some people a more or less full-time concern. There was much acrimonious debate over academic issues (e.g., course offerings, course contents, hiring decisions, etc.) and these debates only became more complicated, political, and fractious with the founding of what came to be known as the departmental Assembly.

I will not enter into a detailed discussion of the politics behind the passage of the departmental Constitution and the founding of the departmental Assembly, though Professor Giffen's essay provides an excellent starting point.[6] Suffice it to say, the Constitution established a set of policies and procedures for the governance of the department, instituting a form of direct democracy. The key mechanisms of the new system were the departmental Assembly and a system of parity committees. In the Assembly, each person, from an undergraduate student taking one course to a full professor, was accorded one vote. Policy and other decisions were decided under the guidance of Bourinot's *Rules of Order*.[7] Though decisions were not binding on the Chair, there was an expectation that they were to be attended to very closely.[8] Decisions made in the departmental committees, all of which were run on a parity basis (e.g., equal numbers of students and faculty), were likewise "advisory"—but not to be ignored. It was an interesting experiment, but for all the benefits it produced in terms of democratizing departmental governance, there were serious short- and long-term costs: a decline in interpersonal and professional civility among the department's citizens, huge losses in administrative efficiency, and, as the chairs point out, a clear diminution of the department's reputation in the university.

This system of governance was in place in 1972 when Irving Zeitlin took over the essentially impossible task of running the department. As his account makes clear, these forces and factors—scholarly, academic, political, personal, and societal—influenced the daily business and civic culture in the department during his tenure as Chair. As with Jim Giffen's chairship, it was a period of heated and seemingly intractable political debates and confrontations. Its legacy would influence the department for years to come.

I will not presume to "tell the departmental tale" for the years 1970 to the present. The essays do that—if in a partial way and from a particular point of view. Instead, I invite readers to engage the essays to follow on their own terms; that is, as *post hoc* accounts written by well-respected senior scholars with a particular perspective on a complex set of events unfolding over four turbulent decades. I will conclude by making a few, highly selective observations about the University of Toronto's Department of Sociology. Between 1963 and 2003, Canadian society changed with astounding rapidity. For its part, the Canadian university system was transformed three times, first by rapid, massive, government-funded growth, then by retrenchment, and finally, by a restructuring which has rendered it vulnerable to the influence of corporate agendas. Canadian sociology in general, and Sociology at the University of Toronto specifically, tagged along. The discipline expanded rapidly coincident with general growth in the universities and then had to deal with the same problems of retrenchment and restructuring that came to face the system as a whole. In the process of growing and becoming professionalized, sociology became infinitely more varied and complex in terms of its theoretical and methodological conventional wisdom(s), and political practices. Also, more than ever before, it became a research-intensive enterprise. All of this influenced the department at Toronto, and as a large proportion of the current Sociology faculty retires over the next decade, it will be interesting to see what new changes occur.

One of the most striking things about the set of essays to follow is that for all their differences in tone and subject matter they highlight a relatively small number of key issues. First, each of the chairs operated under the premise that the Toronto department, as the "flagship" department in the country, had an obligation to offer an inclusive, "cutting edge" curriculum to its graduate and undergraduate students. This is tied to a second common view, that the department has always been, and remains, a highly productive research-oriented enterprise—again, perhaps, a model for the Canadian sociological community as a whole. This means that, third, throughout its history, the department has expended a great deal of energy attempting to recruit and retain top-notch faculty. But, at times, these three goals have been jeopardized.

In the 1960s, 1970s and even into the 1980s, political wrangling was an enormous problem. Many of the scholarly-political debates that characterized the era were healthy and inevitable; a consequence of legitimate differences of opinion about the proper form that sociological practice should take. Healthy, too, were debates over the proper form of departmental governance. But as Giffen, Zeitlin, and Marsden point out, at Toronto these intertwined debates became so personal and vitriolic (especially in the 1970s) they created a civic culture that, at times, challenged the department's ability to function to its full capacity as a center of teaching and scholarship.

Another key problem in the department, one of more recent origin—and by no means exclusive to Toronto—is the difficulty of finding sufficient funds to carry on the academic enterprise. Zeitlin had little to say about it, but in the accounts provided by Professors Simpson and Tepperman, money is a paramount concern. Operating budgets, money for sessionals and teaching assistants, competition for external research grants, financial resources to establish research chairs, etc.—these are the new terms of reference within which the department has increasingly operated. Given its professed desire to be a "world class" department within a "world class" university, these are also the terms of reference within which it must build a future. As Lorne Tepperman put it: "We are now trying to play in the big leagues, and in the big leagues, research dollars have been a problem for a long time—perhaps forever. Perhaps that what makes the big leagues big."[9] Research and teaching remain the department's key priorities. There is no doubt it does not wish to relinquish its status as Canada's "flagship" department, especially in regards to research activity. But funding difficulties now far outweigh problems of civic culture as the department's primary concern.

I suspect that the story of the department for the foreseeable future will depend on its success in finding the money to recruit and retain top-rank Canadian and international faculty and students within this kind of environment. Certainly, the relative balance of the sources from which the department attracts the funds it needs—(e.g., government grants, targeted donations from private corporations and individual philanthropists) will have a tremendous impact on who gets hired, what aspects of Canadian and international social reality get researched, and what subjects constitute the core of the curriculum.

As a student of the history of Canadian sociology, I was extremely pleased to have been involved in the production of *A Quarter-Century of Sociology at the University of Toronto, 1963-1988*. I knew it would be a remarkably useful research tool and it occurred to me at the time that similar volumes about the establishment of each of Canada's departments of sociology would be equally valuable. What a boon such a library would be to historians of sociology and the social sciences. The present volume, produced on the fortieth anniversary of the department's establishment, confirms my belief that the 2003 book, even more than its predecessor, will come to hold an important place in the history of Canadian sociology.

NOTES

1. I would like to thank Anne Mitchell and Professors Dennis Magill, Lorna Marsden, John Simpson, and Lorne Tepperman for their comments on drafts of this paper. I am responsible for any errors of fact or interpretation it contains.

2. Professor David Brownfield served briefly as Chair in 1996, before a medical emergency made it necessary for him to leave office.

3. Over the fall and winter of 1997-98, I conducted interviews with Professors Zeitlin, Marsden, Reitz, and Simpson regarding their respective periods as department Chair. Transcripts of these interviews will soon be available in the Department of Sociology Archives housed in Robarts Library.

4. He co-wrote an introductory sociology textbook heavily influenced by human ecology (Dawson and Gettys, 1929, 1935, 1948), hired Chicago

graduates (most notably Everett Hughes and Aileen Ross), and, like his colleagues and students, carried out research on typical "Chicago School" topics: immigration, ethnic relations, and patterns of urban life. In addition, he extended the empirical reach of human ecology to a non-urban setting by carrying out a series of studies of pioneer settlement and ethnic assimilation on the Prairies (1934, 1936, Dawson and Younge, 1940). Also notable were the results of the McGill Social Science Research Project directed by the Fabian Leonard Marsh, also at McGill. Regarding the McGill Social Science Research Project, see Irving (1986) and Shore (1987). Regarding Marsh's contribution, see Wilcox-Magill and Helmes-Hayes (1986), and Helmes-Hayes and Wilcox-Magill (1994), as well as a number of essays in the *Journal of Canadian Studies* 21(2), 1986.

5. The classic overview of the history and basic premises of the new political economy is Marchak (1985).

6. Many of the papers that would be required to undertake such a task are available in the Department of Sociology Archives housed in the Robarts Library. Likewise, many of the individuals involved are still available to be interviewed.

7. Lorna Marsden noted in comments on a draft of this paper that she brought about a change to Roberts' *Rules of Order* when she became Chair. She noted that Bourinot's assumes a daily Parliament with continuity of membership, a party structure (with an Opposition), and an impartial speaker. Roberts' was seen as more suitable for the department's community assembly approach.

8. As Zeitlin points out in his essay in this volume, it was not until he assumed the chair that the Assembly voted to make all committees parity committees. Prior to that time, the Staffing Committee had been the exception.

9. From Professor Tepperman's comments on a draft of this introduction.

REFERENCES

Axelrod, P., *Scholars and Dollars*. Toronto: University of Toronto Press, 1982.

Braverman, H., *Labor and Monopoly Capital*. New York: Monthly Review Press, 1974.

Canada, Dominion Bureau of Statistics, *Canada Year Book 1963-64*. Ottawa: Queen's Printer, 1964.

Canada, Royal Commission on the Status of Women, *Report*. Ottawa: Information Canada, 1970.

Clark, S.D., *The Social Development of Canada*. Toronto: University of Toronto Press, 1942.

_______., *Church and Sect in Canada*. Toronto: University of Toronto Press, 1948.

_______., *Movements of Political Protest in Canada, 1640-1840*. Toronto: University of Toronto Press, 1959.

Cormier, J., "Nationalism, Activism, and the Canadian Sociology and Anthropology Community, 1967-1985," *The American Sociologist* 33 (1) 2002:12-26.

Dawson, C. [with the assistance of R.W. Murchie], *The Settlement of the Peace River Country*. Toronto: Macmillan, 1934.

_______., *Group Settlement*. Toronto: Macmillan, 1936.

Dawson, C. and W.E. Gettys, *An Introduction to Sociology*. 1st, 2nd and 3rd eds. New York: Ronald Press, 1929, 1935, 1948.

Dawson, C. and E. Younge, *Pioneering on the Prairie Provinces*. Toronto: Macmillan, 1940.

Eichler, M., "Feminism and Canadian Sociology," *The American Sociologist* 33(1) 2002: 27-41.

Harrison, D., *The Limits of Liberalism*. Montreal: Black Rose, 1981.

Helmes-Hayes, R. (ed.), *A Quarter Century of Sociology at the University of Toronto 1963-1988*. Toronto: Canadian Scholars' Press, 1988.

Helmes-Hayes, R. and D. Wilcox-Magill, "A Neglected Classic: Leonard Marsh's *Canadians In and Out of Work*," *Canadian Review of Sociology and Anthropology* 30(1) 1994:83-109.

Hiller, H., "The Canadian Sociology Movement: Analysis and Assessment," *Canadian Journal of Sociology* 4(2) 1979:125-50.

_______., *Society and Change*. Toronto: University of Toronto Press, 1982.

Irving, A., "Leonard Charles Marsh and the McGill Social Science Research Project," *Journal of Canadian Studies* 21(2) 1986:6-25.

Jones, F., "Establishing the Canadian Sociology and Anthropology Association (CSAA)," *Society/Société* 14(3) 1990.

Journal of Canadian Studies 21(2) 1986.

Leacy, F.H. et al. (eds.), *Historical Statistics of Canada*, 2nd ed. Ottawa: Statistics Canada with the Social Sciences Federation, 1975.

Macpherson, C.B., *The Real World of Democracy*. Toronto: CBC, 1965.

_______., *Democratic Theory*. Oxford: Clarendon Press, 1973.

_______., *Property*. Toronto: University of Toronto Press, 1978.

Magill, D. and Michelson, W. (eds.), *Images of Change*. Toronto: Canadian Scholars' Press, 1999.

Marchak, P., "Canadian Political Economy," *Canadian Review of Sociology and Anthropology* 22(5) 1985:673-709.

Miliband, R., *The State in Capitalist Society*. London: Weidenfeld and Nicholson, 1969.

Nock, D., "The Chicago Imprint in Canada: Oswald Hall and S.D. Clark," J. Foraker-Thompson (ed.), Proceedings of the 28th Annual Meeting of the Western Association of Sociology and Anthropology, Boise State University, Boise, Idaho, 1988.

Owram, D., *Born at the Right Time*. Toronto: University of Toronto Press, 1996.

Pentland, H.C., *Labour and Capital in Canada, 1650-1860*. Toronto: University of Toronto Press, 1981.

Porter, J., *The Vertical Mosaic*. Toronto: University of Toronto Press, 1965.

Shore, M., *The Science of Social Redemption*. Montreal and Kingston: McGill-Queen's University Press, 1987.

Thompson, E.P., *The Making of the English Working Class*. Harmondsworth: Penguin, 1963.

Wilcox-Magill, D. and R. Helmes-Hayes, "Leonard Charles Marsh: A Canadian Social Reformer," *Journal of Canadian Studies* 21(2) 1986: 49-66.

Wipper, A. (ed.), *The Sociology of Work*. Ottawa: Carleton University Press, 1984.

How the Department of Sociology Came into Being

How the Department of Sociology Came into Being

S.D. CLARK

By stretching a point it could be said that sociology had its beginning, at the University of Toronto at least, in 1915. It was in that year that R.M. MacIver joined the faculty of the university. As a lecturer in political philosophy at the University of Aberdeen before coming to Toronto, as he relates in his autobiography, *As a Tale that is Told*, MacIver had developed a strong interest in sociology and his continued interest in the area while at Toronto was evident in the extended revision of his sociological study, *The Community*. It was only after moving to Columbia University in 1927, however, that he gained recognition as a sociologist. At the University of Toronto all his teaching was in the area of political science, and he appears to have had no influence upon the later development of sociology at this university.

To E.J. Urwick belongs the credit for the establishment of a teaching program in sociology at the University of Toronto. After retiring from the London School of Economics and Political Science as a professor of social philosophy, Urwick had come to Canada with the intention of settling in Vancouver (he was a man of private means). However, a bitter struggle between two senior professors for the headship of what was then known as the Department of Political Science on MacIver's leaving led Sir Robert Falconer, the president of the university, to persuade Urwick to assume the post. Soon after, he was also appointed Acting Director of the School of Social Work, then known as the Department of Social Science, a position he was to hold (as a result of the prolonged illness of the director) until his retirement from the university.

It was primarily to provide a background of training for students entering social work (then a one-year diploma program after the B.A.), which led to Urwick's interest in 1933 in establishing an Honours program in sociology. To anyone not familiar with the thinking in the university at the time it might appear strange that an Honours course in sociology was set up before there was a single person in the school to teach the discipline. But among the founders of the course, including Urwick (and the new president of the university, Canon Cody), sociology was not thought of as an independent area of study; rather, it was conceived of as a distinctive grouping of a number of different areas: political science, philosophy, history, psychology, anthropology, and zoology. A committee was established to administer the program, made up of faculty members drawn from these different areas of the university, with Urwick as chairman.

No sociology was offered in the first year of the program. Students with the intention of honouring in sociology took courses in what was known as social and philosophical studies. As the first cohort of students moved into the second year, however, it was necessary to secure someone to teach a course in Introductory Sociology. C.W.M. Hart, a lecturer in anthropology, with a strong interest in sociology, was given this task.

If Urwick, with his strong background in social philosophy, had doubts about the claims of sociology as a science, those doubts were not shared by Hart. Brought close to the great master of sociology, Emile Durkheim, through Radcliffe-Brown, Hart taught a rigorously positivistic and functionally oriented sociology to his students in Toronto. It was not the kind of sociology which found favour in many quarters of the university. In Victoria College, because of the moral relativism in Hart's teachings, students were put under heavy pressure by the registrar to avoid entering the sociology Honours program. Hart, however, very much the charismatic teacher, quickly gathered a following among those students who came in contact with him, and the effect of his teaching was to establish the discipline of sociology as a recognized area of study within the university. Though it was Urwick who brought into being the Honours program, to Hart should go the credit as the founder of sociology as a discipline at the University of Toronto.

In 1937, the first body of students graduated in Honours sociology. By then the staff could be considered as consisting of three persons: C.W.M. Hart, E.J. Urwick, and David Ketchum. Hart now taught a fourth year as well as second year course in sociology and, while still holding an appointment as Lecturer in Anthropology, had been named as Supervisor of Studies in Sociology. Urwick, rather curiously described as Professor of Economics, taught a fourth year course on the history of social welfare. Ketchum, an Assistant Professor of Psychology with a Ph.D. in social psychology and sociology from the University of Chicago, offered a fourth year course on human ecology. In addition, engaged in the final year of study for my Ph.D., I was called upon to teach a third year course on the history of sociological theory (the only course in sociology yet offered in the third year). Together with these five courses, students were required to take, after social and philosophical studies, courses in economics, economic history, psychology, history, philosophy, anthropology, and zoology. There were no options. In offering a broad range of training, it was a truly excellent Honours program.

Until 1938, no one teaching courses in sociology except J.G. Franz, an instructor for the year 1937-1938, held a teaching appointment in sociology as such. Hart was in anthropology, Ketchum in psychology and Urwick in political economy. To begin in 1938, however, it was decided by the committee in charge of the Honours program to appoint a full-time lecturer in sociology. The result of the deliberations that ensued determined to an extent the direction sociology was to take in its development in the university. E.A. Bott, head of the Department of Psychology, proposed the appointment of one of his students who was taking his Ph.D. in sociology at the University of Chicago. My appointment, with a year of teaching at the University of Manitoba coming to an end, was proposed by H.A. Innis, head of the Department of Political Economy. Had Bott succeeded, sociology at the University of Toronto, like that at McGill at the time, almost certainly would have come under the influence of what at the time was known as the "Chicago school" of sociology. But Urwick, the chairman of the committee in charge of the Honours program, disliked Chicago sociology. As a consequence, acting on Innis' advice, he recommended to the President my appointment as a lecturer in sociology.

The future of sociology in the university, however, was not thereby wholly resolved. As a university lecturer, I had to be attached for administrative purposes to a department (only departments had budgets). Since Hart's appointment was in anthropology, it was decided to attach me to the same department. All that this meant, however, was that my salary became part of Anthropology's budget. It was to Urwick rather than to the head of the anthropology department, T.F. McIlwraith, that I was actually responsible. To make still more ambiguous my position, I was assigned an office in the old McMaster Building on Bloor Street occupied by the Department of Political Economy, a goodly distance from anthropology's quarters in the Royal Ontario Museum, which could be reached only by means of the main door on Queen's Park Crescent.

Already as well, however, Hart's position was becoming increasingly ambiguous. All the teaching in sociology was carried on in the McMaster Building, and it was in this building that Hart came to have his main office. To neither of us, as a result, did the relationship with anthropology appear to make sense. It was to Innis, head of the Department of Political Economy, that we tended to turn for academic advice. Accordingly, sometime late in the year 1939, we approached him with the proposal that sociology should be incorporated in his department. The proposal, when put before the Honours course committee, met a not wholly favourable response. Some of the members of the committee, with unkindly feelings toward what was considered "the empire of political economy," were of the view that sociology should become a separate department. In the end it was decided that for a period of two years the Department of Political Economy be put in charge of sociology. After two years the committee would meet again, when consideration would be given to the establishment of a separate department.

What the members of the committee failed to take into consideration was that in approving the transfer of sociology (including the responsibility for the supervision of the Honours program) to political economy, the committee as such ceased to exist. The only person who could have re-convened it was Urwick, its chairman, and before the two years were up he was no longer with the university. An attempt on the part of other members of the committee to raise the question of the place of sociology in the university would have been considered an intrusion into the affairs of the Department of Political Economy, and Innis was not the kind of person to brook such an intrusion. It was, thus, more than twenty years before any further serious consideration was given to the creation of a Department of Sociology.

Sociology, on its transfer to political economy, did not thereby lose its stature as a distinctive discipline. Now began to emerge what could be considered as a sociology staff. Within two years time there was no one teaching a course in sociology who did not hold an appointment in the subject. Hart became an assistant professor of sociology rather than of anthropology. Ketchum in 1941 ceased to teach the fourth year course on human ecology which he had been offering, though he continued to teach in the Department of Psychology a third year course on social psychology which Honour students in sociology were required to take. Urwick retired from the university, now finally settling in Vancouver. I was joined in 1940 by E.G. Devereux, a student of Talcott Parsons in Harvard, who was appointed an instructor in sociology—appointment as an instructor was simply a means of avoiding the payment of the $1,800 minimum salary for a lecturer.

Our location for the first four years on the northeast corner of the second floor of the McMaster building gave the staff in sociology a sense of being an autonomous group. We had our own Honours program, which remained distinct from that of economics and political science. Later we had, as well, our general course program. A steadily growing program of graduate studies leading to the M.A., and ultimately to the Ph.D., was organized and directed by the staff. Only in one important regard was the autonomy of sociology limited. It did not have its own budget, and what funds were available for new appointments were determined by the head of the department (as were salary increases). While sociology faced the constraints of the departmental budget, the staff in sociology was given an almost completely free hand in recommending new appointments.

The 1940s and 1950s were not years of rapid university growth and the slow expansion of the staff in sociology was a reflection of this fact. After two years at Toronto, with the United States now in the war, Devereux in 1942 was called up by the American navy, his place taken by Aileen Ross, who remained on the staff for the next three years before returning to her hometown, Montreal, and McGill University. The hiring of Eva Younge in 1943-1944 and D.G. Marshall in 1944-1945 as sessional appointments allowed Hart and me to secure the teaching of sociology's complement of honours courses. The building up of what might be described as the regular staff began in 1945 with the appointment of J.R. Burnet as an instructor who, after spending the year 1948-1949 at the University of New Brunswick, returned to Toronto as a lecturer. Her appointment was followed by that of P.J. Giffen in 1948 and L. Zakuta in 1952. S.M. Lipset spent the first two years of his teaching career at Toronto (1946-1948), and Eli Chinoy, the first four years (1947-1951). For the three years 1951-1954, Norman Ryder was a member of the staff, and for the two years 1951-1953 J.C. Riemersma from Holland who, with training in both chemistry and the social sciences, went on from Toronto to Berkeley to teach economic history and then returned to his native land to take up his research interest in the field of chemistry. Also holding appointments in sociology in 1950-1954, but without salary, were J.R. Seeley and R.A. Sim who, holding a mental health research grant from the federal government, were on the staff of the Department of Psychiatry while carrying out the Crestwood Heights study. Hart left in 1948 to accept an appointment at the University of Wisconsin, and in 1956 Oswald Hall joined the staff to be followed by N. Keyfitz in 1959, H.K. Nishio in 1961, and R.C. Beals, R.A. Lucas and D.E. Willmott in 1962. In addition to such distinguished visitors as Robert E. Park, Talcott Parsons, R.K. Merton, Helen McGill Hughes, and C.A. Dawson, Theodor Geiger was a visiting professor in 1951-1952, Sir A. Carr-Saunders in 1960-1961, and Morris Ginsberg in the spring term of 1948. In 1962-1963, the staff consisted of eight full-time members. Keyfitz was on leave that year, to accept an appointment at the University of Chicago the next year, while Nishio, to comply with U.S. immigration regulations, did not take up a regular appointment at Toronto until 1964. Though his name appeared on the staff list as a special lecturer, R.J. Coughlin was in fact a member of the faculty of newly established York University, which, for the year 1962-1963, under the conditions of its founding, was affiliated with the University of Toronto. Coughlin did, however, take part in a monthly staff seminar held on an informal basis in the homes of different members of the faculty.

With Vincent Bladen, C.A. Ashley and W.T. Easterbrook coming after Innis, the staff in Sociology was fortunate in its Chairmen (now no longer known as heads). There were distinct advantages in being a part of Political Economy. While Sociology's image may have suffered in some quarters outside Toronto as a result of its seeming lack of independence as an administrative unit, the tie with Political Economy very much enhanced its image within the university. The department was one that was highly regarded in the university administration. The gain to Sociology was particularly evident in the development of its graduate program. In contrast to proposals from some departments, proposals going forward from Sociology to the School of Graduate Studies generally gained ready acceptance. There were other advantages as well in being a part of Political Economy, not the least of which was avoiding the administrative chores involved in the management of a department.

If the tie with Political Economy served to strengthen the position of Sociology in the University of Toronto, in many ways it served as well to strengthen its position in the Canadian academic community at large. While Toronto Sociology may well have been looked at askance in some sociological quarters, its standing as a discipline was greatly enhanced from its association with such highly regarded scholars as Harold Innis. The first appointments in Sociology in Saskatchewan, New Brunswick, and Victoria College in British Columbia were of persons who had done their graduate work in Toronto. As well, close ties were established with McMaster University and the University of Manitoba.

One of the major activities undertaken by the staff in Sociology was the establishment, with a grant from the Rockefeller Foundation, of a two-day seminar which met once a year over a three-year period, beginning in 1955, devoted to a discussion of a major issue in sociology. Sociologists were invited, with their expenses paid, from the different universities in Ontario and Quebec. Also attending were some people from federal government departments. The first seminar was built around the subject of population, with Kingsley Davis as a special guest. There followed a seminar on elites with C. Wright Mills in attendance, and one on small-group sociology with George Romans. It was at the last meeting of the seminar that steps were taken to organize the sociology chapter of the Canadian Political Science Association, a development that led ultimately to the establishment, in 1965, of the Canadian Sociology and Anthropology Association.

Throughout the years leading up to the establishment of the department in 1963 members of the staff were engaged in a number of research studies. It was while at Toronto that Lipset carried to completion his study on agrarian socialism and Chinoy his study of automobile workers. Burnet, following up on her study of an Alberta rural community, turned to a concern with the relationship of systems of moral values to the changing structure of the Canadian society, while Giffen turned from a study of the legal profession to an interest in studying deviant forms of behaviour. Zakuta moved from a study of the C.C.F. in Ontario to an examination of interpersonal relations in society. Hall, after coming to Toronto, followed up on his study of the medical profession to the general area of the sociology of work while Keyfitz carried forward his work on South East Asia. My own interest in the development of the Canadian society led to studies of sectarian religious movements and movements of political protest in Canada over time, and to a study of the suburban society.

At various times before 1962, in no very serious way, the question was mooted whether Sociology should become a separate department. The respective chairmen of Political Economy—Innis, Bladen, Ashley, and Easterbrook—were not in favour of separation, and no move was made by members of the Sociology staff which would have led to such a development. The close personal ties which over the years had become established between the members of the Sociology staff and other members of the staff in the Political Economy department, more particularly on the part of the younger members of the department situated on the fourth floor of the old McMaster Building, had built up very much a sense of community. On academic grounds, the view was strongly held by the department of the value of the close association between economics, political science, commerce and finance, and sociology.

In the course of the year 1962-1963, however, a marked change occurred in the position of Sociology in the Department of Political Economy. The department had, in 1960, taken up quarters in Sidney Smith Hall and, with the expansion now beginning to occur in the university, it grew to over one hundred and fifty staff members. It took one of the largest rooms in Sidney

Borden Building, 563 Spadina Avenue, Department of Sociology 1963-1990
PHOTO: JEFF REITZ

Smith Hall to accommodate a faculty meeting. Members of the Sociology staff, scattered as they were on the third floor among economists, political scientists, and commerce and finance people, began to lose a sense of belonging to a community.

It was, however, a development outside Political Economy that precipitated the move that led to the establishment of a separate department of Sociology. By 1963, Sidney Smith Hall had become so crowded that it could no longer accommodate all the departments that had been housed there in 1960. Volunteers were called for to move to the Borden Building, which had just been taken over by the university. Given some interest on the part of the members of the Sociology staff in making such a move, Oswald Hall and I paid a visit to the building. The only way we could gain entry was by crawling through an unlocked basement window. Our not unfavourable report led to the decision to inform Dean Bladen that we were prepared to make the move. Sidney Smith Hall, with its windowless inside offices and at the time without air conditioning, held little attraction for its occupants. Eventually the Departments of Anthropology and Islamic Studies were asked by the Dean to move with us. We were assigned accommodation on the second and third floors of the building, with the university police occupying the first floor.

In moving to the Borden Building, the expectation was that we would remain a part of the Department of Political Economy. Once the planning of the office accommodation in the building was underway, however, the awkwardness of the situation became apparent. The President of the university, Claude Bissell, had made it known that he thought Sociology should become a separate department, and a chance discussion between Hall and me led to the discovery that we both favoured such a move. There followed a meeting of all the members of the staff in the main lounge of the faculty club and it was decided to seek the establishment of a separate department. Accordingly, Hall and I met with Easterbrook, the Chairman of the Department of Political Economy, and Bladen, the Dean of the Faculty of Arts and Sciences, to convey the views of the Sociology staff. Easterbrook was very much against Sociology moving out of Political Economy, holding the view that economic history required its presence in the department to offset the growing dominance of theoretical economics. Bladen, however, in his usual decisive manner, acted on the request of the Sociology staff and recommended to the President the establishment in the university of a Department of Sociology.

The department came into being July 1, 1963, with myself as Chairman, and Mrs. Sorenson as Secretary. We took up our office quarters, together with Anthropology, on the second floor of the Borden Building, with Islamic Studies located on the third. All that remained was the establishment of the department's budget. The university budget for the year 1963-1964 had already been passed by the board of governors. It was necessary, therefore, for the dean to transfer to Sociology some of Political Economy's funds. For 1964-1965 Sociology secured its own budget. By then the staff had grown to fifteen people; this growth was to continue unabated for the next ten years.

Some Recollections of Sociology in Two Universities: McGill and the University of Toronto

Some Recollections of Sociology in Two Universities: McGill and the University of Toronto

OSWALD HALL

In the preceding chapter, S.D. Clark has documented the steps through which sociology at the University of Toronto became an official department. By an interesting coincidence, Professor Marlene Shore, in her recent volume *The Science of Social Redemption*, has traced the early decades of the Department of Sociology at McGill, in particular the formative period, 1920-1940. Since these two departments soon became the leaders of sociology in Canada it is of interest to compare and contrast how the subject gained a place in each university. In other words, how did the larger enterprise, sociology as a realm of research and a field of teaching, become established as an enduring part of these universities?

In attempting such a comparison I have depended on a set of personal recollections. These range in age from half a century to a quarter of a century, and are often the worse for wear. As noted above, the efforts of Clark and Shore are based on archival records, and stand at the other pole as far as documentation is concerned. The best I can claim is an effort to use a sociological perspective to maintain a depersonalized view of the emergence of these two departments.

During their formative years these two departments of sociology had minimal contacts with each other. Geographical distance and the demands on time and energy contributed to an "arm's-length" relationship between them. On the other hand, this was not true of the two universities. On this larger scene there was vigorous rivalry between the two institutions. This was especially marked between their respective schools of social work, each of which played a consequential role in the emergence of sociology and its efforts to establish a distinctive identity.

Forty years elapsed between the establishment of a department at McGill and one at Toronto. That at McGill emerged during the post-war Depression of the 1920s, and developed its distinctive character during the Great Depression of the 1930s. That at Toronto began to take form during the Great Depression, but achieved formal status only later, during a period of prosperity and optimism on the Ontario scene.

The issues addressed in this essay can be summarized as follows. In what ways can its distinctive urban environment impinge on an emerging department of sociology? What are the peculiar circumstances faced by the discipline as it finds acceptance in the academic community? How does a consensus arise as to what will be taught, and be the subject of research, in the new discipline? In what ways can the teaching enterprise be structured to transmit the discipline to future generations? What administrative arrangements in the university facilitate the growth of a new discipline? And what are the elements of morale and *esprit de corps* that favour the success of the sociological enterprise?

THE URBAN SETTINGS

The place of sociology at McGill tended to mirror the place of McGill in Montreal. McGill is a private university, an orphan child as far as the city of Montreal and the province of Quebec are concerned. The department, like the university, was perpetually short of resources, both physical and budgetary. The struggle for survival was genuine.

On the other hand, Montreal was a laboratory tailor-made for sociological research, especially for those who enjoy studying society "on the hoof." It was a city with a cosmopolitan flavour and a readily grasped structure. Mountains and rivers hemmed it in, thus denying it the luxury of the urban sprawl so common on this continent. Its geography and history had combined to make it a grand hub of water and rail transportation. History had endowed it with the great head offices of finance, commerce, and industry, which in turn dominated the affairs of half a continent.

Like many other North American cities it was a product of migration. The new population groups had generated an elaborate social structure. On its map the two dominant groups, Francophones and Anglophones, were sharply divided by an unmarked line. Within these two divisions there had emerged enclaves of minority groups. The shoulders of the mountain (Mount Royal) tended to parallel the social classes of the city. Where residential areas collided with commercial areas one could readily locate the human casualties of city life: the poor, the unemployed, the disorganized, and those on the wrong side of the law. Economic classes and social classes all had a recognizable location in the structure of the city.

The city of Montreal presented intriguing research queries for a sociologist. How and where do migrant newcomers find a place to settle? How do they attach themselves to work opportunities? How do they prepare their children for such challenges? How do racial, ethnic, and religious minorities maintain (or surrender) their cultural bonds? How do they sort and sift themselves with respect to the occupational and industrial structure of the city? Montreal was both an intriguing social laboratory and an exciting cosmopolitan city in which to live.

Toronto, as the locale for an emerging department of sociology, presented a vastly different visage. It could hardly claim cosmopolitan status. Rather, it retained much of the character of a provincial town. On the other hand, it gave promise of enormous sprawl to the east, the north, and the west. Moreover, it was marked by strong population growth, particularly of European migrants, in the wake of the Second World War. But with the exception of a Chinatown, any sharply defined areas of ethnic concentration scarcely existed. Where they could be detected, they tended to have rapidly shifting borders. Toronto lacked the tiny enclaves of ethnic and religious groupings, which Montreal exhibited (and which invited sociological attention).

On closer observation it was evident that while Toronto had not become a cosmopolitan city, it was on its way to becoming a metropolitan centre. Unlike Montreal, it had developed as the hub of a constellation of smaller cities. Whereas Montreal was essentially self-contained, for Toronto much of the relevant commerce and industry was dispersed in a system of encircling communities. General Motors to the east and Ford to the west had generated distinctive satellite cities. Hence Toronto was essentially the centre of an increasingly large constellation of vigorous and wealthy communities.

Moreover the University of Toronto was also on the way to becoming the centre of an increasingly large constellation of universities and colleges.

While McGill, as a private institution, was fundamentally a product of a narrowly based upper class in Montreal, and had generated hostile relations with the government of Quebec, the University of Toronto was a provincially supported institution. Moreover, the Ontario government was increasingly disposed to support education in general, and this support flowed toward universities. While McGill routinely faced a bleak future with regard to financial support, the University of Toronto suffered little in the way of such constraints. It could afford a department of Sociology.

Without stressing the point unduly, it can be confidently asserted that the geographical setting helped define sociology in the two universities. At McGill the classical problems of urban sociology lay bare to view on the body of the city, within reach of a streetcar ride. At Toronto they were scattered and concealed in a metropolitan community, its satellite cities, and its extended hinterland.

THE EMERGENCE OF SOCIOLOGY

On both campuses one can trace early tentative steps to establish Sociology, as well as the official efforts to find it a place in the university. At Toronto two developments are noteworthy—the creation of an Honours course in sociology in the 1930s, and the establishment of an autonomous department three decades later. At McGill these two developments were telescoped.

It is usual to equate the beginning of Sociology at McGill with the name of one man, Carl Dawson. He came to McGill at a point when the School of Social Work was struggling over the relative importance of research and social action. Others outside the school were also involved in the struggle, persons in administration, and economists such as Stephen Leacock. (As a matter of record, his *Sunshine Sketches of a Little Town* was first-class small town sociology.)

Marlene Shore was much impressed by Dawson's crusading zeal for sociology and his single-minded efforts to create a department dedicated to teaching and research. She attributed his congenial conversion to sociology as a product of his Baptist background, since she saw in that religion a ready affinity with scientific orientations. A more convincing argument can be made that Dawson was deeply influenced by sheer mobility—both his own and others'. His early background was that of the most stable social system in Canada—Prince Edward Island. Family systems and farm family systems had there generated a secure environment. The years that Dawson spent later in the Western prairies, as a school teacher, were a vivid contrast. Incidentally, he returned there a decade later to study systematically the family systems and settlement processes that had earlier attracted his attention. The impact of the First World War, and his experiences with returning soldiers, contrasted vividly with the security of his own early years. Later, when he went to the University of Chicago, he encountered a tumultuous, impersonal city. Previous observers had noted that "City air makes man free." This it did for Dawson. There he developed an intensely interested, but highly detached, concern with urban life, freed of attachment to any enterprise except sociology. Other teachers at McGill could become embroiled in social movements, reform movements, and political movements, but he created for himself a core of scholarly detachment.

Although he was saddled initially at McGill with the administration of the School of Social Work, he quickly shed those responsibilities in order to concentrate on Sociology. His strategy was two-fold: to emphasize the teaching of sociology with a Canadian flavour, and to pursue research into what he considered consequential problems on the Canadian scene. In his eyes the two enterprises were interlinked. Because there were few teaching materials at hand, he co-authored an introductory textbook, one that had a durable academic life. Thereafter, he engaged in research, particularly with respect to the dynamics of Canadian population growth, and movements and the settlement of new parts of Canada. On a large canvas he promoted research through the activities of the Social Science Research Council and the cooperation of philanthropic foundations. As time went on very useful teaching materials emerged, such as E.G. Hughes' *French Canada in Transition* and Horace Miner's *St. Denis*. For his own part, Dawson generated a series of general articles as well as four volumes on Western Canada.

In the sociology courses which he generated at McGill the research interest blended with the teaching interest. The students were encouraged and challenged to explore the society around them, and to view it through a sociological lens. Initially there were two foci of this enterprise. Students were stimulated to explore, in a detailed way, the families of which they were a part, and also to explore the distinctive neighbourhoods in which they participated. For most of these students, sociology became a much more lively enterprise than the book learning which they encountered in most other departments.

The interest in sociology was most lively and intense among students who registered in the Honours program. In those courses student interest pyramided upon student interest, and as a result there was a steady growth in graduate courses leading to the M.A. degree. The research interest helped to create the degree, which in turn placed major emphasis on the research thesis. The graduate students became field sociologists who created substantial research documents while at the same time arming themselves for significant careers as sociologists. In the latter years of his life at McGill, Dawson could savour the success of his research-teaching career. The late 1940s saw an impressive cohort of graduate students, a large number of who later chaired departments of sociology.

The emergence of Sociology at the University of Toronto has been chronicled by Professor Clark, but it may be useful to pursue comparisons with McGill. If at McGill the genesis of the department partook of the nature of an immaculate conception, at Toronto the metaphor would be that of a protracted Caesarean section, perhaps the longest on record.

At McGill the Sociology program emerged as an effort to achieve academic distance from Social Work; at Toronto it was designed as an important supplement of social work teaching. Slowly and gradually this bond dissolved, both as an administrative arrangement and as a focus of teaching. Initially those teaching Sociology were drawn from a variety of fields, and worked under the umbrella of the Department of Anthropology. Eventually the teaching staff comprised solely sociologists, but by this time they worked under the Department of Political Economy.

At McGill Sociology was represented by someone who was, by training and conviction, undoubtedly a sociologist. Dawson had studied at an impressive department of Sociology (the University of Chicago), and was ranked as one of its top graduates. He had a sturdy sense of being an authentic representative of his discipline, and he determined, as the department grew, to add only recognized sociologists of comparable stature. By contrast, the Toronto venture began by collecting a team of teachers. These were of diverse backgrounds, including an anthropologist, an economist, and a psychologist, plus Professor Clark, who had studied undergraduate history, proceeded to the London School of Economics, and moved to McGill to study sociology for two years. After seven years the economist and psychologist were dispensed with. The anthropologist continued for another seven years, by which time the program was an unambiguously sociological enterprise. Unlike Dawson at McGill there had been no initiating figure to impose a homogeneous character on the program. To a large degree the sociologists took guidance from the larger department, one which encouraged a high degree of freedom for teachers to devise their own courses.

THE SOCIOLOGY CURRICULA

The structure of a department is little more than a framework around which the program coalesces. The formation of a new discipline in the university rests on the recognition of a new participant in the division of labour in the field of knowledge. It also rests on a degree of consensus among the teachers in that field as to what the core of the new discipline comprises.

As noted above, the program at Toronto was by its nature eclectic. The four initiating teachers brought diverse backgrounds to the common task. Since the objective at the beginning was to supplement the training of social workers, a broadly based set of courses was readily justified. The range of interests of the instructors was impressive. One member brought an orientation from social philosophy, with a European flavour. Another had trained in anthropology, with a focus on preliterate peoples. The third was a professional psychologist who had developed an interest in human ecology during his studies at the University of Chicago. The fourth brought a broad acquaintance with Canadian society, and with his background in history, political science, and sociology, could be properly described as an historically oriented social scientist.

While such an array of courses could well serve the needs of students in social work, they were untidy bedfellows as far as an authentic Department of Sociology was concerned. As time went on only one of these orientations survived, that of historically oriented sociology. As the others disappeared from the program, formally trained sociologists with an acquaintance with the Canadian scene took their place. Thereafter, the students in Sociology had the opportunity to explore such fields as population, minority groups, political movements, and legal and health care systems. As mentioned earlier, these developments took place within a Department of Political Economy, one which encouraged the intermingling of a variety of disciplines, and which also provided a maximum of autonomy for teachers to create their own distinctive courses. Hence there was little pressure to generate a "Toronto school" of sociology.

The contrast with McGill has been foreshadowed in the preceding section. At McGill sociology was no adjunct of social work, but rather a repudiation of any such ties. It also turned resolutely away from the "Social

Problems" view of sociology as a study of crime, delinquency, suicide, prostitution, poverty, and such matters. Dawson viewed sociology as a thoroughly autonomous field of study with its own foci of attention and the corresponding obligation to carry out research therein.

Very early in his work at McGill he co-authored an introductory textbook which indicated the directions in which the department would evolve. His central course work would concentrate on the community, particularly the urban community. To this would be added courses on population and migration of peoples. Whereas these courses would reflect an ecological approach, they would be supplemented with courses dealing with culture. Eventually teachers of cultural anthropology would be added to the department. (In Toronto these were separated in distinctive departments.) At McGill there were further courses to be added dealing with the family (Dawson originally taught this course), and courses on the socialization of the child in the family. Dawson also pursued this field in the direction of adult socialization, in his course on social attitudes. While all of these courses can be viewed as an integrated view of a society, Dawson also realized that there are dramatic and even revolutionary changes occurring, which may shatter the structure of a social system. Hence courses were added in the general field of social movements as a counterpart to those just described.

Note was made earlier of the teaching orientation of courses in sociology at McGill—the dual emphasis on library work and field study. Students were exposed to the classical literature insofar as the library resources permitted, but were vigorously encouraged to supplement this approach by an attempt to gather raw data as an integral part of the sociological enterprise. Dawson held the notion that "to be a sociologist is to know something about something." In his eyes, well-grounded knowledge emerged from field research. This emphasis tended to put sociology in a special place on the campus, since most other departments relied almost entirely on library resources. This dual orientation in sociology had a salutary effect on the work for the M.A. degree. For that program, all students were required to complete a dissertation based on empirical data. In other departments and in other universities, students could obtain this degree by course credits solely. The McGill policy regarding the M.A. program contributed greatly to the reputation for research in general which the department enjoyed.

THE TEACHING ENTERPRISE

The teaching of sociology at McGill had something of a collective character, both in the planning of courses and in the teaching and assessing of students. This could be noted on three levels. The large courses, in which there were various sections, were organized on a unified framework of common readings. All students would end up with a roughly comparable background in sociology, as a prelude to succeeding courses. While each teacher generated his or her own teaching style, there was a sturdy common core. Students and teachers had a common understanding of what each course entailed.

In these courses, use was made of graduate student teaching assistants. These met students to discuss both reading materials and the term projects noted earlier. They also participated in the grading of reports and examinations. This arrangement required close collaboration among the assistants as well as with the relevant faculty members.

Further collective energy went into the planning of the curriculum as a whole, and the integration of its parts. Where faculty enjoyed a common background in their own graduate work this was easily managed. Where their backgrounds differed, as occurred when social anthropologists and sociologists devised a common course, the collaboration was more arduous. The result, it was hoped, was a more unified course rather than one in which the integration of materials was left up to the student.

The manner of teaching the courses determined in large part the manner of assessing students. The assessments occurred at various stages in a course and involved, in large courses, several staff. Term projects formed an integral part of the overall assessment of the student. It was difficult for a student to get lost, or be anonymous, in such circumstances. The grading system stood at the opposite extreme from the true-false and multiple-choice examinations that were arising in other departments in the university.

In Sociology at Toronto there seemed less emphasis on joint planning of courses and the integration of teachers. To some degree this pattern arose in the very beginning, when scholars of diverse orientations each contributed a course. Moreover the ethos of the Department of Political Economy, to which sociologists belonged, strongly emphasized the individual prerogatives of faculty members to create courses on their own initiative. On the other hand, the actual evaluation of grades of final examinations was eventually a collective affair, with marks passing up through a series of committees. Hence idiosyncracies in grading by specific instructors would be counteracted.

One peculiar feature of the Toronto examinations was the system of anonymity under which students wrote. Hence it was officially impossible for the instructor in a course to discover the identity of the student writing the examination. As a consequence, a teacher was precluded from seeing, at the end of a course, the progress of a student along the various stages of that course. This arrangement had stemmed from peculiar historical circumstances, and like much else would disappear around the time the department was formally established.

THE CONTEXT OF ADMINISTRATION

Professor Clark has discussed the early incorporation of sociology in the Department of Anthropology at Toronto. Soon afterwards it found a home in the Department of Political Economy, which comprised economic history, economic theory, and political science. This was a congenial home with a large family of cognate subjects.

It was also a prestigious place to locate. The senior members of the department enjoyed superior reputations as scholars, and thereby added an enviable environment for the new discipline. The head of the department was an internationally acclaimed social scientist, and at the same time an energetic administrator. His research scholarship was a challenge to members of the new discipline, and his administrative skills left the sociologists free of such chores. To this should be added his role as Dean of Graduate Studies. His encouragement made it easy for the Sociology department to establish a graduate program at an early stage.

The larger department provided a model for the recruitment of new members of the teaching staff in Sociology. While the department sought, as occasion arose, to attract luminaries from other campuses, it also found a place for its own promising graduate students. It would be incorrect to stress unduly the role of selection from within. In large part, the department provided teachers for an encircling set of comparable departments in other parts of Canada. Later these scholars might return to Toronto, having proved their competence in a different environment.

The availability of contact with other members of a heterogeneous department meant that sociologists were not restricted to fellow sociologists for companionship. Small departments tend to breed intense personal relationships, but Toronto sociologists escaped this hazard.

The generous welcome to a large department of a small body of newcomers eventually had unanticipated consequences. By the time the sociologists were prepared to go their own way they had become so important to some parts of the larger department that their going was deplored.

The incorporation of Sociology at McGill took an entirely different turn. No department offered to take it under its wing. The established departments were either actively hostile to the new discipline, or questioned its credentials in a negative way. Each step on the road to acceptance had to be earned either through student recognition or by contributions to research. Moreover, this was in effect a one-man enterprise. There was no counterpart to the four-man team that pioneered sociology at Toronto.

If Dawson viewed his work as something of a crusade, some of his students soon came to share this enthusiasm for the place of the new discipline. When the opportunity came to participate in research on the settlement of Western Canada, Dawson was in the enviable position of having a research orientation that was much in demand and having a first-hand acquaintance with the area to be studied. While he made no converts among the economists involved in that research, he won grudging respect from some of them.

As Dawson looked forward to the expansion of the department he insisted adamantly on adding only established sociologists. He fought to secure colleagues rather than junior assistants. In this he battled against the recruitment policy of other McGill departments, and the vigorous opposition of deans and other administrators, who, with an eye on the budget, preferred appointments at the most junior level. Dawson aimed at an egalitarian colleague framework for a department, rather than a hierarchy of levels.

The department that he created lacked the luxury of a benevolent umbrella such as that enjoyed by sociologists of the University of Toronto. Hence Dawson had to seek out kindred spirits in the university in whatever department he could find them. There was a core of them who enjoyed fishing, skiing, and vigorous conversation. This group was expanded to include pivotally important members of the Faculty of Arts, who in due course would support Dawson's goals for his department.

That department grew from very small beginnings. One result was an atmosphere that promoted the growth of very warm collegial relationships. Professor Clark has mentioned the spatial dispersal of faculty members in the early history of Sociology at Toronto. At McGill the members worked in close physical proximity. Moreover, spouses and other family members came to share in the life of the department, even including teaching chores. The newly recruited members joined a warm cohesive group. The candidates for new positions visited the campus as house guests rather than hotel guests. Meal-sharing and evening parties were a norm. Day-long picnics, which included graduate students, became a veritable institution. The graduate students in turn formed their own lively seminar groups to supplement, and on occasion subvert, the formal arrangements.

In conclusion, it is clear that the McGill and Toronto departments moved toward their present levels of prominence by markedly different routes. In this essay a few of the important contingencies have been noted. The surrounding locale in which the university is set grants some opportunities and excludes others. Historical developments in other parts of the university impinge on the development of a new discipline. The legacy of those who initiated the new enterprise continues to provide direction far into the future. The emerging understandings as to what constitutes the core of a discipline, and the core activities of its representatives, constrains the development of a department. The administrative arrangements within which a department is nestled impose an imprint on that development. And, finally, the inner ethos and *esprit de corps* which accompany its emergence maintain a lingering influence on its future development.

Through the Eyes of the Chairs

Department of Sociology Chairs
(Back row, left to right): Lorna R. Marsden, Jim Giffen, John H. Simpson, Lorne Tepperman. (Front row, left to right): Jeff Reitz, S.D. Clark, Irving M. Zeitlin.

In preparation for this volume, Professors Giffen, Marsden, Reitz, Simpson, and Tepperman were asked to provide a brief essay describing the primary issues during the time they served as Chair. The responses we received follow.

We hope that these responses will reflect the fascinating working environment that has existed in the department throughout the years, and will showcase the department's unique role in fostering excellence in teaching and research.

Rick Helmes-Hayes
Dennis William Magill
Anne Mitchell

S.D. Clark
Chair, 1963-1969

Samuel Delbert Clark is known as the "Dean of Canadian Sociology." When the Department of Sociology was established on July 1, 1963, he was its first Chair. In his essay in this volume, Clark describes how the department came into being. The "founding" sociologists, i.e., those in the department at the time, were Ralph Beals, Jean Burnet, S.D. Clark, Jim Giffen, Oswald Hall, R.L. James, Rex A. Lucas, Doug Pullman, D. Reuschemeyer, Don Willmott, and Leo Zakuta.

During the six years that Clark was Chair, the department grew very rapidly. By 1969, the year he stepped down, there were 35 faculty members. The graduate department had grown very rapidly as well.

Professor Clark's work is well recognized by his peers. A number of books have acknowledged the great significance of his career and scholarship. Foremost among these books are: *Society and Change: S.D. Clark and the Development of Canadian Sociology* (Harry H. Hiller), *The Limits of Liberalism: The Making of Canadian Sociology* (Deborah Harrison), and *Images of Change* (Dennis William Magill and William Michelson, eds.) His legacy at the Department of Sociology is immeasurable.

Jim Giffen
Chair, 1969-1972

This brief but turbulent period was notable for its excessively participatory democracy. The student-power movement and the simultaneous push among faculty for a greater role in decision-making, pandemic in California, reached the frozen north while Del Clark was still chairman. Three professors circulated an open letter calling for a faculty meeting to consider the creation of a more democratic system of decision-making. At the meeting it was resolved that a committee be elected to propose a constitution for a form of participatory democracy. And then, true to the temper of the times, it was stipulated that the committee should include an equal number of students. This addition of "parity" completed the populist pantheon and launched us on a slippery slope.

The task of constitution-making was unbelievably time-consuming. The members of the ten-person committee, with alternating faculty and student chairmen, jostled for advantage while pooling their ignorance. However, the voting on contentious issues was rarely an even student-staff split. Some faculty members, perhaps sensing the shape of power to come, sided fairly frequently with the student bloc. Two faculty representatives, alarmed by what seemed to be a reckless rush to give away the store, emerged as the resident neanderthals. It should be emphasized, however, that nobody advocated a return to the status quo; times had changed, and so had the range of possibilities. The gentle reader will be spared a blow-by-blow description of the proceedings, in part because I can't remember the details (one of the few advantages of old age).

If we had deliberately set out to do so we couldn't have devised a system better suited to wasting time and fostering discord. The radical dream had spawned a dystopia. The centrepiece was the Assembly, made up of all the faculty and an equal number of elected students, presided over by the unfortunate Chair. As might be expected, this proved to be a splendid vehicle for the discharge of aggression at a time when little encouragement was needed. At the initial session I suggested that we follow Bourinot's Rules of Order, the procedural guide for the House of Commons. Given the affinity at the time between radicalism and chauvinism, this was an easy sell. The fact that I had bought the only copy in the bookstore brought me a short-lived illusion of mastery.

When Del Clark's time as Chair came to an end in 1969, I was asked to serve as Acting Chair during the search for a successor. After a misleading honeymoon period, some of my colleagues apparently decided I was doing my best with the convoluted populist script. A draft movement limped through the corridors of the Borden Building and I, unhinged by the implied flattery, agreed to a three-year term, counting time served. The Dean and some of my colleagues promised strong support. Harry Nishio, the Associate Chair, agreed to stay on during the transition period.

Elected parity committees now made the decisions in all the major areas of administration except staffing. The exclusion of students made this a focus of discontent throughout the period. The belief that university regulations made appointments and promotions entirely a matter for faculty and administrators prevailed for the next three years, and may have helped make this our most effective committee. At the first meeting we were faced with an embarrassment of riches—over a hundred applications for teaching posts, mainly from newly minted Ph.D.'s and ABDs who swore that they were trembling on the brink. A sub-committee was appointed to do a first winnowing, and we arrived amiably at a short list. The political ideology of candidates was almost never an issue (this came later).

The growing popularity of sociology courses (some of the titles were pretty sexy) strengthened our claim for tenure-stream appointments. When Woodsworth College approached us about having some faculty on their masthead and offered to pay two salaries, we agreed on four cross-appointments, thus expanding our own tenure-stream complement by two more than the number the Dean had granted us (he was not entirely amused). This agreement did not affect the number of our courses available to Woodsworth students, or who taught them.

Time has shown that several of the new colleagues who favoured us with their custom in 1970-1973, and stayed the course, have contributed significantly to the common enterprise. If one were given to name-dropping (heaven forbid) one might mention John Kervin, Dennis Magill, Lorna Marsden, Jeff Reitz, Janet Salaff, John Simpson, and Meta Spencer (if you're missing, feel free to sue). Some others left for greener and more peaceful pastures.

If memory serves, my amicable relationship with the Staffing Committee necessitated remedial sneakiness on only one occasion. We had voted to recommend three Associate Professors for promotion to full Professors but had failed to get the stamp of the Executive Committee. This procedural slip provided the occasion for a palace revolt in the Assembly, where the Chair was sat upon. When it next met, a chastened Staffing Committee voted to eliminate one of the recommendees, despite my objection that this meant discriminating between two equally deserving colleagues. The Dean and I discussed the problem and agreed that the loser would appeal to him and that the appeal would be granted. This was done, but at the cost of needlessly humiliating a valued colleague. I had the impression that the members of the Staffing Committee, to their credit, were somewhat relieved by the outcome.

There was no "game plan" at the beginning of this reign of idiocy, merely a desire to survive each day's challenges. However, after an endless round of committee meetings following the same pattern of reporting, discussing, drinking coffee, moving motions, and voting, I began to think that others might be getting tired of it. Since I was already committed to living by the constitution, extra zeal could not be construed as subversion. So, we played the participatory democracy game to the hilt, meeting and meeting again, discussing many banal matters that could have been looked after administratively. It would be gratifying to report that at the end of three years a demand for less participatory governance had emerged, but no such luck. The explanation seems to be that it was mainly the most politicized of our constituents who were highly involved in departmental affairs, and it was precisely they who were least likely to countenance what seemed to be a step backward. The majority simply went about their business.

A big change in our undergraduate program at this period came in response to developments in the Faculty of Arts and Science. The Dean, Bert Alien, appointed a committee made up of a student and a faculty member from each department—some forty souls in all—to examine the B.A. program. Student dissidents had been highly critical of what they (and

The Varsity) called "the mind-fuck curriculum," and professors lecturing on subjects with political relevance had been heckled ("fanonized") in the classroom. In Arts and Science, and particularly in Sociology, the university had, for the time being, ceased to be an institution of civility.

In the committee's endless discussions the students tended to pursue two general goals: (a) to maximize freedom of choice in selecting courses, and (b) to minimize any elitist connotations in the designation of degrees. The traditional Honours programs fell short on both counts. These programs (in geography, history, sociology, etc.) made certain courses mandatory, and required choices to be made from specified groups of subjects, the object being to combine specialization with a liberal education. The graduates were identified as having an Honours B.A. in their special field. As usual, the students on the committee were not alone in wanting a change. The outcome was "The New Program," a giant intellectual cafeteria instituted in 1969, whose fluid compromises with specialization need not concern us here. Students could now expose themselves to permanent damage from an overdose of sociology. Within the department a lot of effort was involved in bringing our own undergraduate requirements into line while providing for the students who were finishing under the old program.

It is one of the anomalies of university administration that an academic can be appointed as a chairperson responsible for planning and administering a budget in the seven-digit range without anybody even inquiring whether he knows his way to the nearest bank machine. Fortunately most academics are quick-study artists, and have access to expert advice. Sociology was saved from insolvency by our Administrative Assistant, Jean (Brownie) Joyner, who was, among other things, a whiz at fiscal affairs and the very model of an administrator. (She was also a part-time lecturer whose evening course on organizational theory was highly popular.) It helped in balancing the books that the Dean was relatively generous to Sociology at budget time.

Advising students on academic matters is of course central to the teaching role, but it is those who do this officially in combination with the requisite paperwork who have the awesome task of saving students from their worst impulses. They were known at the time as the Undergraduate Secretary and the Graduate Secretary (later, when it was realized that they couldn't take dictation, they were given grander titles). From the beginning, we were blessed with excellent front-line administrators. Sad to say, I can't recall who they were and can find no printed record. Egocentricity brings to mind Leo Zakuta's tenure because he succeeded me as Graduate Secretary when I was chaired. Our greatest contribution to the efficient administration of graduate studies came when we hired Jeanette Wright, as generations of students and their supervisors will attest.

Dress was an important part of revolutionary symbolism; the Ivy League model was replaced by lunch bucket proletarian. Whereas the standard for males in academe had been jacket, slacks, tie, and shoes, the new fashion statement marked the abandonment of couth: jeans, preferably scruffy, lumberjack shirts, and clumpy boots. This attire first became standard among dissident students and gradually spread to younger faculty who wanted to be identifiable as part of the gang. For our tiny cohort of female colleagues there didn't seem to be a marked change; perhaps more slacks and fewer dresses. We old male troglodytes continued to dress as if we were going to church.

In the end the department survived, with some difficulty but more or less intact. Despite the distractions, we met our classes, exploited our teaching assistants, recruited some splendid new colleagues, and even did some research and writing. And when the pot smoke settled we thought we could see a better road ahead.

Jim Giffen

Irving M. Zeitlin
Chair, 1972-1977

I was recruited as Chair of the Department of Sociology in 1972, a time when the political tumult of the 1960s, far from having diminished, had augmented. The war in Indo-China continued to rage, and in some respects increased in scope and intensity, while the Civil Rights movement, which had its beginnings in the United States, expanded to embrace many other countries. The women's movement for equality also gathered momentum at the time. What, therefore, could have been more natural than for the spirit of that era to have animated the discipline of sociology in general and the U of T department in particular?

Indeed, before I arrived, the spirit of the era had profoundly influenced and transformed the Toronto department. The old U of T tradition, in which departments were ruled by Heads appointed by the administration, was challenged, and a revolution occurred. The Head, S.D. Clark, was effectively deposed, and a new form of departmental government, based on a new code of laws called a Constitution, was established.

When I arrived, the new departmental government, chaired by Jim Giffen, had already been in effect for two or three years. And it was my responsibility as the newly recruited Chair to navigate the department through this tumultuous era.

The departmental Constitution provided for student parity on all committees except the Staffing Committee, and for a General Assembly in which any student, enrolled in at least one Sociology course, acquired voting rights in both the Assembly and on committees. During the first few weeks of my term as Chair, the Assembly, by means of a two-thirds majority, amended the Constitution to provide for student parity on the Staffing Committee as well.

The reader might wonder why I had agreed to chair the department under such circumstances. As a candidate for the Chair, I was required to present a colloquium to the department. Following the colloquium, I was asked the explicit question of whether I would be willing to serve as Chair under the new Constitution. I replied that though I failed to see any philosophical or moral justification for granting students authority equal to that of faculty, I would be willing to work with the Constitution as a social experiment. However, I also made it clear that I would do so only as long as it was generally understood that I was the president and chief executive officer of the department and, therefore, the final authority where major departmental policy decisions were concerned. The administration also insisted that all concerned accept this principle. Despite my reservations regarding the parity system, I was selected over several other candidates, and I learned that I had received the largest number of votes from each constituency in the election—faculty, students, and staff.

It wasn't too long after I had arrived and assumed my duties that I discovered the extreme political polarization of the department. On the one side, I found the "old guard"—the older, senior people who were almost unanimously opposed to the parity system. S.D. Clark's attitude was fairly typical in that regard. In a personal conversation with me he once remarked: "Can you imagine what has been wrought here under that so-called Constitution? A student who takes one Sociology course has authority equal to mine. We both have one vote!"

On the other side, in contrast, I found those whom I shall call the "radicals"—the younger faculty and the students. Given the polarized condition of the department, I found myself trying to mediate between the two factions: the "old guard" urging me to nullify the Constitution and the parity system, and the "radicals" wanting me to preserve it and to recruit new faculty sympathetic to the system. Of course, so strongly held were the opposing views that my efforts at mediation were rarely successful.

THE COMPOSITION OF THE DEPARTMENT

There were, at the time, at least sixty colleagues in the department if we include the suburban campuses, the Clarke Institute, and the Criminology Centre. It was a large department, but a large proportion of the faculty consisted of ABDs (All But Dissertation), a fact which nobody had apprised me of prior to my arrival. How such a state of affairs had occurred might best be explained by describing the then prevalent recruitment policy of the university and the department.

The Canadian university system was then in the midst of a period of unprecedented and rapid growth. The society was experiencing an extraordinary increase in the number of students desiring higher education, and as the pool of academically trained Canadians was presumably too small to accommodate both the large volume of students and the expansion of Canadian universities, a policy of recruiting faculty from the elite universities of the U.S. was instituted. U of T search committees turned primarily to Harvard, Yale, Princeton, Berkeley, and other such elite schools to recruit the most highly recommended Ph.D. students; it was quite common for them to be hired before having completed their dissertations. In our department there were about a dozen such colleagues who had been appointed some five or six years prior to my arrival and who, for whatever reason, had not yet completed their doctoral dissertations and were about to face tenure proceedings.

This situation threatened to become a real crisis in the department, if each and every case were not assessed with a care and justice evident to all concerned. It was an especially delicate situation because the time when an M.A. was considered a professional academic degree had pretty much passed, and the administration had let it be known that it would not countenance the granting of tenure to ABDs unless they had refereed publications to compensate for the lack of a Ph.D.

Moreover, these candidates for tenure had to satisfy two committees, not one as in other departments. There was the decanal committee and there was a parity committee required by the Constitution. The decanal committee was composed exclusively of faculty and a dean or his associate, while the parity committee consisted of students and junior (i.e., pre-tenured) colleagues and senior faculty. I participated in the meetings of both committees and read most of the materials submitted for consideration by the candidates for tenure. It soon became clear that most of them were not only far from completing their dissertations, but also that they had no refereed publications to their names. In these circumstances, the denial of tenure was virtually unavoidable. This outcome was naturally a sad and painful moment for all departmental members, and it was no consolation to the failed candidates that both the decanal and the parity committees had concurred in their decisions.

RECRUITMENT

One of my chief responsibilities as Chair was to help in the moulding of a first-rate department where scholarship and high-quality teaching were concerned. The recruitment of promising young and distinguished senior faculty was therefore our paramount aim. Under the Constitution, the search committee was elected from the student and faculty bodies, and was composed of an equal number of representatives from each constituency. I participated in all of the meetings of the search committee. After reviewing the credentials of the prospective candidates, the committee drew up a list of candidates to whom I ought to make an offer. In each case, I agreed with the committee's recommendations and the result was that we successfully recruited eight new faculty members. It so happened, however, that although some of the new recruits had already been on the faculties of other Canadian universities, only one or two was either born in Canada or a naturalized citizen. This came to be a major problem, for at the time there was immense pressure on Canadian universities to hire Canadian citizens. Canadian citizens comprised less than 40 percent of Sociology faculty across the country, and in the early 1970s a movement arose to "Canadianize" faculties, curricula, and textbooks. Canadian departments of Sociology, including the Toronto department, were producing a relatively large number of Ph.D.s, and the University of Toronto was pressured to hire its share.

When it became known at the 1974 meeting of the CSAA that U of T had hired so many non-Canadians, someone offered a motion to censure our department. I learned on the day following the meeting that faculty members of our department, including members of the search committee who were responsible for drawing up the list of candidates to whom an offer was to be made, had voted for the censure. And this despite the fact that the censure tended to lay the entire responsibility for the hiring decision at my door. Only one member of the search committee came to me after the event to apologize for the committee's hypocritical behaviour.

MORE ON THE PARITY SYSTEM

In order for the reader to gain an adequate grasp of the workings of the department at the time, I need to say a few more words about the Assembly and the parity system. The Constitution was a document consisting of several pages outlining the authority structure of the department. The document was only occasionally consulted, but every student, new and old, and every faculty member knew that its central principle was student parity on all committees. It was in the General Assembly that we considered the business of the several committees, and where we considered issues that colleagues or students wished to air before a larger audience. The Assembly ratified the decisions made in the respective committees. During my term as Chair I cooperated fully with this experiment in participatory democracy, but as soon as my term ended and Lorna Marsden occupied the Chair, she let the Constitution die a natural death by convening the Assembly seldom or not at all, and by either working with the committees or ignoring their existence, in accordance with her wishes. In the first two years of her chairmanship the entire system ground to a halt and became defunct. There were no more Assembly meetings after that.

During my term as Chair, however, the parity system carried with it considerable intra-departmental strife, as well as unfavourable publicity throughout the university community. Almost daily the department's doings were a central topic of the university's media. In the *Varsity* and in other publications we often found letters from disgruntled "radical" graduate students for whom we were not democratic enough; at the same time it became generally known that some of our senior colleagues, who frequented the Faculty Club daily, were saying very unkind things about the department.

The atmosphere became so unpleasant that I seriously considered resigning from the Chair. I approached Dean R.A. Greene early in the second year of my term, informing him that, although I was willing to remain on the faculty as a plain professor, I wished to resign as Chair. Giving me a disturbed look, he asked me to reconsider, explaining that the reason they had searched for a Chair outside the department was that they could not agree on an internal candidate. The university, he stressed, was certainly not about to incur a large expense again searching for an outsider. "What can I do," he asked, "to persuade you to remain in the Chair?" I replied that as a consequence of the political turmoil in the department I was neglecting my scholarly work and atrophying intellectually. I told him I had in mind a project for a book, and that I might be willing to continue in the Chair if he could give me a full-time administrative assistant. That way I could devote myself to research in the mornings, and chair the department in the afternoons. Fortunately, there were funds readily available in those days; he agreed, and I was able to start an important project and to feel like a scholar again.

THE CHAIR AS INTELLECTUAL GUIDE

The political strife in the department made it virtually impossible to create a common intellectual telos. The committee that had recruited me explicitly stipulated that they expected me to provide some form of intellectual leadership, and I had hoped to provide it, drawing upon my previous experience, first, at Indiana University and, then, at Washington University in St. Louis. At Indiana University, I was active in teach-ins and in a faculty organization called the Continuing Committee, about fifty colleagues who literally saved the university from being burned down during a period of racial strife. Members of this organization mediated between the black and white student radicals on the one side, and the administration on the other. There is no time or space for the full story, but one of our major accomplishments was to persuade the administration to refrain from calling in the National Guard and from taking extreme measures against the students.

When I was recruited to the Washington University Department of Sociology in 1970, I was not surprised, given the continuing political turbulence of the era, that Alvin Gouldner and others wanted to create in the department, together with its sister disciplines, a mini-Frankfurt School specializing in what was dubbed "critical sociology." Although the meaning of that phrase was not entirely clear, the central idea was to develop a critical approach to all the institutions of society. In discussions of the phrase and its programmatic implications, the question was much debated whether one can be critical and at one and the same time objective in Max Weber's sense. To many of us at the time, criticism and objectivity seemed to be reconcilable.

When I came to Toronto, I was still enamoured of the possibility of pursuing scholarly projects in the Frankfurt School tradition. It seemed evident even to scholars not particularly sympathetic to critical theory, that the School and its followers had produced much serious and worthwhile intellectual work. There were, of course, the examples of Adorno and Horkheimer, but also that of Habermas, who was quite active at the time. The question for me and for others in the Toronto department was whether such a sharp focus on a particular scholarly tradition was appropriate for a flagship Canadian department.

It soon became clear to me that what might have been appropriate for a small department, like that at Washington University, was inappropriate for a large department like that of the University of Toronto. It would be wrong, I decided, to try to impart to the Toronto department a one-sided or idiosyncratic character. Although some of the younger departmental colleagues constituted a significant and vocal minority favouring what they continued to call "critical sociology," I decided that our central aim ought to be the creation of a well-rounded and diversified department capable of offering students a good education in all or most of the sub-areas of the discipline. At the same time, however, I had to try to respond to the desires of the "critical" component of the department that wished to recruit scholars working in the "critical tradition." Here, again, I encountered an issue that polarized the department, for it was not only older, senior colleagues, but also junior ones who opposed the program of the so-called "critical" colleagues for being too ideological.

My recruitment policy was one way that I tried to mediate between the two poles. Fortunately, money was readily available for recruitment, and I had the support of both the outgoing and incoming Deans. It was generally understood in the department that certain sub-areas had to be reinforced. It was in that context that we were censured by the CSAA for hiring seven or eight people, most of whom were not Canadian, though they were landed immigrants. Canadian nationalism was at a high pitch at the time, so recruitment also became a contentious issue. On the one side were those who insisted on hiring Canadians rather than outsiders. The proponents of this view argued convincingly that earlier experience with American recruits had shown that they were unfamiliar with Canadian society and history, and they often taught key sub-areas as if Canada were a part of the U.S. The search committee and I therefore did our utmost to recruit Canadian candidates who were equal or superior to non-Canadian candidates. There were, however, instances where it appeared that Canadian candidates were less distinguished than their American counterparts. That was the ground on which we hired the American criminologist, Austin Turk.

At about that time there was a movement, initiated by Norman Bell and several graduate students, to try to hire John Seeley of Brandeis University. There was strong pressure in that direction on the part of some of the more "radical" young colleagues and graduate students. After careful deliberation, I decided not to make him an offer. A rumour was spread that my decision was prompted by strong pressure from the administration. For the record, I need to say here and now that no one in the administration told me not to make Seeley an offer. What some of them did, however, was call my attention to his past performance and history in Canada. Years earlier, he had been recruited by the government to help plan the expansion of higher education in Ontario and in Toronto. At first, the idea was to create a quality, liberal arts college modelled after Swarthmore in the U.S. It soon became evident, however, that given the explosive increase in the number of students aspiring to a university education, the province could ill afford the luxury of investing in a small, liberal arts college. What was needed, the planners decided, was another massive university like the University of Toronto. And, if I'm not mistaken, that was the origin of York University. Seeley, disappointed, opposed the idea, and the result was an acrimonious conflict that left a bad taste in the mouths of the planners. From their standpoint, the least that could be said of Seeley was that he was not easy to get along with.

I agonized over the question of whether to make Seeley an offer, but I soon learned that apart from Norman Bell, not a single senior colleague was in favour of appointing Seeley. Moreover, his *Curriculum Vitae* revealed that he had had very few Ph.D. students in the course of his career. After weighing all of these considerations, I decided against making him an offer. The department, however, needed another senior person of stature, and we had a mandate to hire at least one in the fields of deviance and criminology. I immediately thought of Austin (Ted) Turk, a former colleague of mine at Indiana University, who by that time had distinguished himself as a criminologist.

As I look back upon that period in the department's history, I would have to say that the people we hired during my term as Chair all contributed and continue to contribute to the outstanding reputation of the department. In spite of some of the criticisms of our hiring decisions at the time, I believe the evidence demonstrates that the colleagues hired have made a real, long-term, positive contribution to the department and the university. I need only to list the names of the persons we hired at the time to support the proposition. The list includes Austin Turk who, although he eventually accepted an academic post at a distinguished American university, had contributed substantially to the strengthening of our department's deviance-criminology area. In addition, we hired John Hagan, Lorna Marsden, Michael Bodemann, Bob Mackay, Bonnie Erickson, Harriet Friedmann, and Richard Roman. Several individuals who are now senior colleagues in the department were awarded promotion and tenure during my chairmanship.

MORE ON DEPARTMENTAL DYNAMICS

In the preceding pages, I have made some comments about the "political" condition in the department, and discussed some of the consequences of the polarization that existed. I believe it is important to say more on that subject in a chapter on the history of our department, for there were a number of cross-cutting divisions in the department based on political allegiance, theoretical and methodological orientation, generation, student or faculty status, nationality, and gender.

Perhaps the most powerful divisive force was political or ideological orientation. Some of the younger faculty with an occasional ally from the senior faculty formed, together with certain leaders of the graduate students, a clique or faction in opposition to those whom I have called the "old guard." One of the negative consequences of this ideological conflict was the estrangement of some colleagues who were distinguished scholars and revered teachers, but who identified themselves with neither faction. Such colleagues could find no comfortable niche within the department. Worse, some of them felt "put down," unappreciated, even marginalized. To take just one example that stood out at the time: one highly distinguished senior colleague felt that because of the factions his work was being ignored. Indeed, because his scholarly work did not fit in with or promote the ideology of the "radicals," he felt that they were contemptuous of his research. In a dramatic and moving speech at one of our large meetings, he asked: "Don't you people understand that a human being needs respect? How can a colleague feel good or comfortable in a department such as this, when his work is either ignored or scorned?"

This was a senior colleague who had distinguished himself internationally, and who was not at all associated with the "old guard." Instead, he engaged in a kind of research which, from the ideological standpoint of the "radicals," was not "critical sociology." The radical clique tended to look down upon everyone outside it.

In truth, it would be more correct to speak of two or more cliques or sects rather than one among the "radicals." They were, in fact, split into sects, each claiming to be more "pure," right, or "correct" than the other. This was a phenomenon characteristic of the late 1960s and early 1970s. The "radicals" often tried to out-virtue and outflank one another. If one took a certain position on an issue, one would almost certainly be informed that it was not quite correct, or that the analysis by which one had reached the position was "undialectical" and insufficiently radical. It was fashionable to try to claim greater virtue by taking a position "left" of others. Indeed, when we had read the *Pentagon Papers* at the time, we came to realize that in the North American student movement, there were paid, professional provocateurs who were placed there precisely for the purpose of promoting extreme leftist and/or violent tactics in order to discredit the movement and throw it into turmoil. I confess I suspected at the time that there were a few such elements in our context; but even if those elements were not literally paid provocateurs, their rhetoric and conduct had similar effects.

The problem for the department was that no matter how democratic we endeavoured to be, and no matter what policy decision we reached, it was not democratic enough. Frequently, there was an article in *The Varsity*, and occasionally even in one or another of Toronto's daily newspapers, berating the department or commenting sardonically on its conduct. Naturally, the public pronouncements of the so-called "radical" elements made it easier for the "old guard" to ridicule the constitutional structure of the department when they discussed the department's business with colleagues from other parts of the university. It is a historical fact that as a consequence of the behaviour of both the "radicals" and the "old guard," the department earned itself, in some circles, not respect but notoriety. However, when we consider the history of other social science departments in that era, we recognize that our department was far from unique in reflecting the political and ideological conflicts of the larger society, and indeed, of the international arena.

CURRICULUM CONTENT

Another issue raised in the late 1960s and early 1970s, in addition to the question of whether academic departments could be run more democratically, was whether the traditional curriculum was pedagogically sound. It was a time, for example, when Marx and Marxism were rediscovered in philosophy and in the social sciences, and when certain so-called qualitative methodologies, such as ethnomethodology, became popular. These approaches gained popularity by providing thoughtful, compelling critiques of well-established theories and methods such as functionalism and survey research. As a result of the careful, critical work done in that era, our department, like many others, had to confront curriculum content issues head on.

Pitrim Sorokin once wrote a book titled *Fads and Foibles*, and I think we can appreciate that it is almost inevitable that intellectual fads and fashions will emerge and then decline or disappear, especially in the social sciences and the humanities. An example is ethnomethodology, which was dominant in the department in the early 1970s. It has disappeared now almost without a trace, at least in name, but at the time one could not be taken seriously unless one was something of an ethnomethodologist. Courses were offered on the subject on both the graduate and undergraduate levels, and there were two or three colleagues who specialized in the area.

As for Marx and Marxism, one can easily see why there would have been a renewed interest in that legacy in an era in which certain issues were politically and intellectually salient—issues such as civil and human rights, the emancipation of women, and whether certain wars were just or unjust. I myself taught a course on the history of social thought, using my book, *Ideology and the Development of Sociological Theory*. In the book and in the course, I gave Marx considerable attention, arguing that much of Western sociology emerged in the context of an intense dialogue, encounter, or debate with the ghost of Karl Marx—i.e., with the Marxian legacy. The works of Max Weber, Simmel, Pareto, Mosca, Michels, Durkheim, Mannheim, and others tend to support that proposition. Marxism in some form or other was "in the air" again in the 1960s and 1970s, and several departmental colleagues considered themselves intellectual or methodological Marxists. Although no courses were offered on the history of Marxism, several colleagues offered courses in which the approach was purportedly Marxian. This was true on both the graduate and undergraduate levels. The term "critical" was in large part employed euphemistically to describe an approach in which the Marxian element was central.

Especially among the younger colleagues and graduate students, there was a tendency to employ "Marxism" as an omnibus term embracing Freud, ethnomethodology, the Frankfurt School, and the social construction of reality. In a few cases, the intellectual state of affairs resembled what is going on today among the "post-structuralists." Some individuals took pride in insisting that the distinction between knowledge and ideology was neither valid nor useful. They also cultivated a jargon-ridden writing style that was practically unintelligible. It struck me at the time that the most zealous proponents of such ideas subscribed to a form of moral relativism or nihilism. Academic freedom being a fundamental principle, colleagues taught pretty much what they wished to in the classroom. It needs to be said that there were good grounds for finding the polarization and extreme politicization of issues disturbing. However, it needs also to be said on the positive side that those same conditions created an extraordinarily stimulating intellectual atmosphere in the department. Students seemed quite pleased with the range of course offerings and with course content. Colloquia were presented frequently and, judging from the notable attendance and participation of colleagues and students from other departments, we earned some measure of respect for our scholarly work. The department also went through a couple of academic assessments. The first was done in the early months of my chairmanship, and the second, two or three years later. We came out of both assessments with rather good grades. It would seem, then, that from the standpoint of the assessors we were a well-respected department.

As a result of the assessment and a never-ceasing evaluation and re-evaluation of the graduate and undergraduate curricula, it was generally recognized that as a "flagship" department in Canada, we could not and ought not specialize in only one or two areas. Our explicit mission was to be diverse and offer students the full scope of the discipline. In trying to fulfill that mission, we recruited in a wide variety of areas, striving for a balance between so-called quantitative and qualitative methods.

THE DEPARTMENT'S RELATIONSHIP WITH THE SENIOR ADMINISTRATION

To shed light on the status of the department in the eyes of senior university administrators, I have to return to my remarks regarding departmental politics. As a consequence of the decision of students and faculty members on both sides of the department's ideological divide, the department's political divisions, disputes, and tribulations were often publicized. Senior administrators and members of other departments were thus privy to the turmoil in the department. The result was that neither the department nor the discipline was held in high regard by the university administration. Soon after I arrived, the attitude of certain outsiders and members of the administration reminded me of the British attitude in the early twentieth century: sociology was an upstart and pretentious discipline, specializing in painful and tedious elaborations of the obvious. It had no place in the academy. At the monthly meetings of Chairs presided over by Dean Greene, there was scarcely an occasion where a joke was not made at our expense. In a way, as I've already indicated several times, this was a condition the department had brought upon itself with the frequent letters and articles submitted to the university media by the "radicals," and the equally frequent, unfavourable gossip by senior colleagues in the Faculty Club. The result was a very one-sided and unkind picture of the department that ignored entirely its positive scholarly and pedagogical accomplishments.

I would like to conclude this chapter with a frank and candid evaluation of my accomplishments as Chair in those difficult times. A few years ago, I was interviewed by Rick Helmes-Hayes. One of the final questions he asked was whether I could speak of a major achievement as Chair or a lasting contribution. My most modest reply to that question would be that though I never achieved full success as a mediator, I achieved enough to see the department through several crises, and thus to pave the way for the distinction it has earned under the leadership of the subsequent Chairs—Lorna Marsden, Jeff Reitz, John Simpson, and Lorne Tepperman.

I cannot, however, conclude this chapter of our department's history without giving due credit to Dennis Magill who, in his role as my Associate Chair, contributed mightily to the department's success in overcoming its difficult moments.

Irving M. Zeitlin

Lorna R. Marsden
Chair, 1977-1979

I was quite astonished in the late spring of 1977 to be asked to serve as Chair of the Department of Sociology and, as I look back now, I find it even more astonishing. I had been in the department for only five years, was only just an associate professor, and was very wet behind the ears.

I completed my doctoral degree at Princeton in 1972. The job market, which had been so vibrant in the 1960s, was beginning to close down as the economies of North America went into what became a long period of economic recession in the 1970s. My own research and research interests were not politically radical or fashionable, so I was very pleased when Jim Giffen invited me to a visiting appointment at the department for 1972-1973, and even more pleased when Irving Zeitlin appointed me to a tenure track position the following year.

The early 1970s were politically fraught. A variety of political and social movements—feminism, nationalism, the anti-Vietnam War movement, the U.S. civil rights movement, and others—were blooming, and I was certainly caught up in the women's movement in Toronto—from the fall of 1971, in fact. The women's movement in Canada was divided into factions reflecting the opposition to U.S. influence, but also the range from radical to rights-based action. The department was an extreme version of these movements. Irving Zeitlin was doing his level best to keep the department in some sort of civilized order, but there was a great deal of bullying going on from all sides. Individually my new colleagues were pleasant, supportive, and doing interesting work. Collectively, in the departmental meetings and especially in the Assembly, relations were perfectly awful and made worse by some graduate students who had nothing to lose by personal attacks on some senior colleagues. For a new faculty member still forming academic interests and pursuits, it was both difficult and draining.

I served as Undergraduate Secretary of the Department of Sociology—as undergraduate chairs were called in those days—from 1973 to 1975, and observed the effect of these departmental politics on the undergraduates. A few of the highly politicized became deeply involved. A large number of others, including many excellent students, simply left the department. So, in 1975, it was quite a relief to become Graduate Secretary for the Centre for Industrial Relations where, under the Directorship of the late Noah

Meltz, we were building the Masters of Industrial Relations program. That program required a high level of quantitative skill, balance between labour, management, and public sector interests among the students, and drew on a wide variety of faculty members and courses. It provided a significant contrast to my own department where there was a struggle for intellectual domination, or perhaps simple domination, with the intellectual side subsumed to the sheer desire to win arguments.

I have no idea why, in 1977, the department would suggest that I become Chair when Irving Zeitlin declined another term. It may be that every tenure stream appointee was put on a list and there was a general vote. Certainly I don't recall ever being asked if I would like to stand as Chair. I was very happy to be involved in the MIR program and teaching my own courses in the Department of Sociology. But I do recall meeting Bill Michelson on his bicycle one afternoon as I was walking to the Borden Building. He asked me if I was willing to serve as Chair and when I said "no," he gave me a reasoned but stern lecture about my duty to the department. This shook me up considerably. I did seek the advice of Noah Meltz, who also thought it a good idea, so I suspect that I was a compromise candidate when some deadlock had emerged over more seasoned individuals, and the Dean indicated that no outside candidate would be sought. At any rate, a number of colleagues talked with me and offered to be supportive if I would become Chair. They were all as good as their words about their support.

Of course, I had no concept at all what the job entailed. I had one idea, which was that we needed to "cool down" in the department so that people could get on with their work and not spend so much valuable time on politics. By 1977, the external political pressures had modified and protest was directed more into political parties and established movement groups. A fairly significant number of senior colleagues had drifted away from departmental meetings and committees, but a very large number did attend meetings, serve on appointment and tenure committees, and gave generously of their time and counsel. I developed a great affection and respect for the vast majority of my colleagues in those two years, which continues today. Dennis Magill was always helpful, knowledgeable and prepared to share the work. Jim Giffen's dry cynicism was calming, and Oswald Hall's jokes were unbeatable. Others gave excellent advice, alerted me to problems, and undertook "heavy lifting" on committees. I remain grateful to them.

One issue was quite clear. Both Irving Zeitlin and S.D. Clark left major intellectual footprints on the department and hired excellent faculty. Even had I been capable of leading an intellectual movement in those days, and I was far too young to do that, it was not necessary. My goal was to ensure that a wide range of schools of theory and methods were available to students, and to ensure these programs were able to thrive at a high level of competence.

While the departmental politics were rocky at the start (especially until a great friend in the women's movement gave me a short course on Robert's Rules of Order and the proper conduct of meetings), they calmed down enough for us to get the department business done. The great shock was discovering how the Faculty-level administration was relatively lackadaisical. In one November meeting when they started to discuss appointments for the coming year, I realized that the University was not committed to strategic planning. Each level complained about the next and the blame was, on most occasions, laid at the door of Simcoe Hall. It was not an orderly process—although it changed considerably during my years at U of T to the great credit of a series of deans, the School of Graduate Studies, and the Provost's Office.

Every day was a revelation about budgets, rules, and requirements. Only at the end of my two years as Chair did I discover that all those brown envelopes that arrived were letters from the Dean. I had been throwing them out unopened on the grounds that there was too much mail and if someone really wanted my attention they'd send it in a white envelope. I hope that not too much damage was done by this attempt at efficiency. There were some painful episodes, including denial of tenure to two individuals who I liked a very great deal but who did not make it through the process, and dealing with some personal problems of colleagues. One or two colleagues went around all our processes to get the ear of the Provost or the Dean or the President, and this contributed to the notion that the Department of Sociology was "out of control." I believe that departmental Chair is the toughest job in any university because of the complex interpersonal demands.

We hired some superb colleagues—Harriet Friedmann, Michael Hammond, Richard Ericson, Shelly Ungar, John Hannigan, and Bob Brym. Unhappily, during my second year, Rex Lucas died. He was a greatly valued colleague who had done seminal work in Canada, and was supportive of younger faculty and colleagues—a generous man. At the same time, some excellent graduate students defended their doctoral dissertations in great style, and many of them remain leaders in the field today, including several at York University—Francoise Boudreau-Lemieux, for example, and Paul Craven. One summer afternoon in 1978, just as a thunderstorm broke, a Japanese student, Reiko Sekiguichi, arrived drenched and we discovered

Graduate Seminar—October 17, 1977
Robin Ostow, Lorna Marsden (Chair), Everett C. Hughes, Douglas F. Campbell, Aileen Ross, Dennis W. Magill, Helen MacGill Hughes, Rex A. Lucas, Oswald Hall

that she had a little boy and a very, very young baby, nowhere to live, and the most limited English. Thanks to Claire Campbell, our able Executive Assistant, and some helpful colleagues, she was looked after and she went on to write several important books widely used in Japan about women and girls in Canada and their education. We correspond regularly and that baby, I learned a few weeks ago, is now completing a doctoral degree.

One particularly exciting event during my tenure was the October 17, 1977, Graduate Seminar, organized by the Director of Graduate Studies, Dennis Magill. The Seminar focused on sociological approaches for the analysis of Canadian society. The department provided funds to bring eminent sociologists to U of T to discuss their careers and scholarly contributions. The Seminar focused on the impact of the "Chicago School of Sociology," and was led by Oswald Hall, Everett Hughes, Helen MacGill Hughes, and Aileen Ross. I hosted a lunch at the faculty club, and the photograph shown here has a place of honour on my office wall at York University. (Readers who are interested in the "Chicago School" influence should read Marlene Shore's insightful book *The Science of Social Redemption: McGill, The Chicago School and the Origins of Social Research in Canada*. Marlene, on whose doctoral committee I served, is now Chair of the Department of History at York University.)

When I was recruited by John Leyerle to become Associate Dean of Division II of the School of Graduate Studies in the late spring of 1979, some colleagues were understandably critical of me for leaving so soon. But the department was in good hands with Nancy Howell, a full professor, senior academic, and enlightened leader, who served as Acting Chair and provided a great transition to Jeff Reitz.

The department was really very strong. After I was recruited to the School of Graduate Studies in 1979 and began to compare departments across the university, I realized the disconnection between the low esteem in which our discipline was held within what is a highly traditional university, and the very great accomplishments and orderliness of our department with respect to the areas of recruitment, tenure and promotion, and scholarship. The department continues to have a major influence on the development of sociology and of Canadian society. I'm very proud to have been part of the department and to have had the opportunity to serve as its Chair for that brief period.

Lorna R. Marsden

Jeff Reitz
Chair, 1980-1985

After two years as Chair, Lorna Marsden was appointed Associate Dean, School of Graduate Studies. Nancy Howell acted as the Acting Chair for the academic year 1979-1980. Dean Art Kruger chaired a search committee and Jeff Reitz was selected as Chair. He served from April 1, 1980 to June 30, 1986. His administrative officers were: Bernd Baldus (Associate Chair), Ray Breton (Coordinator of Graduate Studies), and Jim Turk (Coordinator of Undergraduate Studies).

Considerable attention was focused on the graduate program. New options were introduced in the theory and methods requirements. In 1983, an applied Master of Philosophy (Phil.M.) was established. Students were admitted after completing a Master of Arts, or its equivalent. The minimum requirements were three courses and the preparation and final defense of a research paper. The program was intended for individuals who anticipated work as sociologists in private or public industry, government and other non-academic organizations. Due to lack of student interest, the program was discontinued.

Staffing committees continued to be organized along parity, with equal number of students and faculty. New faculty appointed included Charles Jones, Bonnie Fox, and Marion Blute.

Professor Reitz continues to be an active member of the department. In recognition of his scholarship he was appointed to the Royal Society of Canada, and he holds the R.F. Harney Chair of Ethnic, Immigration, and Pluralism Studies.

John H. Simpson
Chair, 1985-1996

By the middle of the 1980s, the Department of Sociology was staffed by a cadre of mostly tenured professors in mid-career. It had significant, recognized academic assets in the fields of urban and community studies, social networks, crime, deviance and socio-legal studies, classical and modern theory, ethnic and race relations, demography, stratification, sociology of religion, family, political economy, gender relations, and methods.[1] Since the late 1960s, it had benefited from the leadership of Jim Giffen, Irving Zeitlin, Lorna Marsden, and Jeff Reitz. It taught a large number of undergraduate students and it had, perhaps, the largest enrolment of students among the graduate departments of Sociology in Canada.

There are various models that have implications for how a department is managed and how its interests are pursued within the university and the external environment. For example, it is possible to view a department of Sociology as, essentially, an organizational weapon enlisted in the cause of some social purpose. My working model was the view that the Department of Sociology was, fundamentally, a vehicle for knowledge generation and transmission. Furthermore, it was my view that this model was best implemented by providing the resources and tools that enabled colleagues with a variety of talents to accomplish the mission of knowledge generation and transmission within the means available. My view is that theory and methods are the heart and head of sociology programs at the undergraduate and graduate levels and that any department of Sociology worth its salt has ongoing population-based research.

The "means available" was not a trivial matter. During most of the time that I was Chair, the department had the highest undergraduate enrolment/faculty ratio (the so-called "Dobell number") of any department in the Faculty of Arts and Science. There was a consistent shortfall in the available funds that could be allocated to budget lines for teaching assistants and appointments. Each year, cap in hand, I begged for money from the Faculty of Arts and Science to pay for TA's and sessionals. When figures for the budget lines of all Arts and Science departments were circulated among chairs by the Dean in the early 1990s, it became evident that differential allocation across departments of, especially, funds for teaching assistants had occurred many years earlier when there was lots of money to pass around. Sociology had not benefited. To be fair, the department undoubtedly had fewer students in the 1960s and early 1970s than it had by the mid-1980s, but the pattern of allocation set in place years before that time remained despite significant growth in Sociology undergraduate enrolments.

By the mid-1980s, the regime of cutbacks in university funding was well established. This had implications for staffing initiatives, and contributed to the rationalization of planning within the university that was initiated by Vice-President and Provost Adel Sedra. At the departmental level, the planning process amounted to devising arguments for keeping positions when retirements occurred. Renewal within the Faculty of Arts and Science was achieved by reallocating retirement vacancies that were not taken back by the Provost in order to effect budgetary reductions at the university level. Throughout this period, the department was successful in maintaining its full-time equivalents with a series of appointments at the assistant and associate levels. Also, there was a small increase in its complement with Jay Turner's appointment in the field of health and medicine, an appointment that was possible because Turner was supported externally as a senior scientist by the federal government's National Health Research and Development Program.

Scarcity of resources also had effects on the delivery of instruction and led to the consolidation of first year Sociology into a single day and a single evening section. There was also a consolidation of the introductory methods courses. These initiatives would not have been possible without the talents and efforts of Bob Brym, Dennis Magill, Bill Michelson, and Lorne Tepperman who at various points took up the instructional challenges of the large courses.

Between 1985 and 1996, and especially toward the end of the period, there was a growing emphasis within the university on obtaining research grants. It was important for the department to be seen as successful in grant competitions, and it was. Those who obtained grants or support from various external sources during the period that I served as Chair included Marion Blute, Michel Bodemann, Raymond Breton, Bob Brym, Doug Campbell, Bonnie Erickson, Eric Fong, Bonnie Fox, Harriett Friedmann, Rosemary Gartner, Ron Gillis, John Hagan, Nancy Howell, Hsiung Ping-Chun, Sev Isajiw, Charles Jones, Jeff Reitz, Janet Salaff, Ann Sorenson, Julian Tanner, Jay Turner, Lorne Tepperman, Barry Wellman, and Blair Wheaton.

I suppose that no former Chair should avoid commenting on parity in her/his mini-report of things past in the Department of Sociology. In a humorous discussion in the halls in the Borden Building, Oswald Hall, one of the most accomplished and delightful figures in Canadian sociology (for my money), once said to me with a twinkle in his eye (knowing full well that I had been a student of theology): "And now abideth faith, hope, *parity*, these three; but the greatest of these is *parity*." By 1985, the importance of parity had come down to equal numbers of faculty and students on the department's staffing committee. By the fall of 1987, there was considerable unease among some Sociology faculty about parity; it was being viewed as an impediment in making desirable appointments, and beyond that, perhaps, as weakening arguments that were made to the decanal office for positions. It seemed time to put the matter to the faculty for consideration.

The decision to have a faculty vote on parity was not taken easily. The risk was departmental turmoil should parity be dismantled. I had been invited to present a paper in the fall of 1987 at a conference on the Caribbean island of Saint Martin/Sint Maarten. The conference was at the same time we were wrestling with the question of what to do about parity. On the flight back to Miami I decided after several cognacs to put the matter to a vote. The faculty voted to replace parity with a procedure for appointing search committees with only faculty members on them. There was no turmoil in the wake of the vote. The *ad hoc* committee that devised the post-parity search procedure included Ray Breton, Bernd Baldus, and Harriett Friedmann as I recall.

Near the end of my first term as Chair, there was an event that led to the departure of the Department of Sociology from its headquarters in the North Borden Building at 563 Spadina Avenue, where it had been housed since its founding in 1963. Most of the space in the North Borden Building—a rundown site originally built to process milk—was occupied by the Department of Sociology, but the rear portion of the building to the east had some members of the Faculty of Forestry in it. One of the Forestry professors had a research collection of small dead fauna preserved in barrels of formaldehyde and stored in the basement of the North Borden Building. In mid-winter, when the ambient temperature in the basement of the steam-heated building probably reached 32 C, one of the barrels began to leak. The smell of formaldehyde was borne to the floors above by rising hot air. It was noxious and in violation of the labour code. Michel Bodemann alerted *The Varsity*. It ran a front-page article on the foul air in the building.

The event led to a meeting in Simcoe Hall with Vice-President and Provost Joan Foley, and the person in charge of university space, Janice Oliver. The dean, Robin Armstrong, was present as was a contingent of Sociology

203 College Street, Department of Sociology 1991-1999

faculty. Sharp words were spoken about the university's long-standing failure to remedy the department's need for decent space. The administration was reminded that every review of the Department of Sociology since it was founded had flagged the problem of space. The upshot was the move of the department to 203 College Street in 1990. The department's administrative assistant, Brenda Mazur, played a significant role in organizing and executing the physical move from 563 Spadina Avenue to 203 College Street.

On July 4, 1996, Dean Marsha Chandler took me to lunch at Prego Della Piazza. (My term as Chair had ended on June 30.) Marsha informed me that the university could no longer afford to rent space for Sociology at 203 College Street. Plans were afoot to move the department to 725 Spadina Avenue where it resides, today, in magnificently appointed quarters.

Academic life in any department oriented to the cutting-edge of research and scholarship always involves presentations by visitors and networking outside the university context. Among the many things that happened in the 1985-1996 period was the development of a connection with colleagues in the universities of Berlin—the Humboldt University and the Free University of Berlin—and also with the University of Bremen and the Technical University of Chemnitz. These connections were initially facilitated by

In 1995, Lorna Marsden received an honourary degree from the University of Toronto—Doctor of Law. The Department of Sociology held a reception to celebrate this event. Lorna Marsden is currently (2003) President of York University. Pictured above from left to right are: John Simpson, Lorna Marsden, and Dennis W. Magill.

Michel Bodemann and led to academic exchanges, workshops and collaborative publications. In the early 1990s, another important connection was made. Professor Nachman Ben-Yehuda, now Dean of the Faculty of Social Science, Hebrew University of Jerusalem, spent the 1990-1991 academic year as a visiting professor in the department.

Some events can have a significant impact on the symbolic standing of a department. Important events in the 1985-1996 period included the appointment of John Hagan as a University Professor and the conferral of honorary degrees by the University of Toronto on S.D. Clark and Lorna Marsden. John Hagan and Bill Michelson were elected Fellows of the Royal Society of Canada, joining Ray Breton, S.D. Clark, Oswald Hall, and Warren Kalbach.

The following were appointed to faculty positions in the 1985-1996 period: David Brownfield, Eric Fong, Rosemary Gartner, Barry Green, Hsiung Ping-Chun, Bill Magee, Ann Sorenson, Gillian Stevens, Jay Turner, Jack Veugelers, Sandy Welsh, and Blair Wheaton.

The following were promoted to the rank of full professor during the period that I was Chair: Bernd Baldus, Michel Bodemann, Doug Campbell,

Charles Jones (Associate Chair, Graduate Affairs), John Simpson (Chair), Dennis W. Magill (Associate Chair, Undergraduate Affairs)

Harriett Friedmann, Rosemary Gartner, John Kervin, Dennis Magill, Ed Silva, and Blair Wheaton.

My terms as Chair overlapped the presidencies of George Connell and Rob Prichard. I had occasion to interact with both of them about various matters. They were friendly to sociology. Dr. Connell was, in my view, the last of the old-style U of T presidents. He had been educated in the elite Ontario system after World War II. His cohort had witnessed and overseen the expansion of the post-secondary system of education that was in full bloom by the mid-1960s. The major premise of the system was that university elites talked with business elites (sometimes) and government elites (often) in order to accomplish what needed to be done to expand the system and keep it running. There was no need to engage mass publics in any sustained way.

By the time Rob Prichard became president, the post-secondary system was (at best) in maintenance mode. Expansion had stopped some years earlier. Cutbacks were becoming routine. Prichard represented a new style of president, a style that required building favourable opinion about the university not only among various elites—especially, business elites—but also among a host of other so-called "stakeholders," including large and small donors and mass publics as well. Development (fundraising) became a rationalized activity, as did public relations. U of T was successfully branded: "Great Minds for a Great Future." In 1996 (when I left the office of the Chair), the University of Toronto was a much different place than it was when I took up an appointment as an assistant professor in 1970.

For most of the period that I served as Chair, I was fortunate to have Charles Jones and Dennis Magill as Associate Chairs responsible, respectively, for graduate and undergraduate affairs. They served the department and the university with distinction. I will always be grateful to them for their loyalty to the department and their good sense.[2]

John H. Simpson

NOTES

1. I have always been reticent to broadcast news within the Department of Sociology about my own field, the sociology of religion. The sources of this reticence were a determination that there was no need to beat the drums for positions in the sociology of religion and given suspicion and prejudice, even hostility, in the discipline directed at religion that there was no point in riling colleagues. There was a *troika* in the department whose work is known in sociology of religion circles: Irving Zeitlin for his books on Jesus and Ancient Israel; Roger O'Toole for his books on sectarian politics and religion and classical sociological theory and, also, various articles on religion in Canada; and my own work—somewhat arcane and technical, perhaps—on high gods, politicized attitudes toward socio-moral issues, religion and the body, and religion and globalization, among other things. O'Toole served a term as editor of the journal, *Sociological Analysis/Sociology of Religion*, and I was president of the Association for the Sociology of Religion in 1995.

2. When Charles or Dennis was on leave, Nancy Howell, who had served a term as Associate Dean of the School of Graduate Studies, took up their duties. Nancy served the department well with grace and aplomb.

Lorne Tepperman
Chair, 1997-2003

ISSUES, PROBLEMS, AND OPPORTUNITIES

For the first fifteen years of its existence, the Sociology department occupied old, cramped quarters in the north wing of the Borden Building. This ancient building had formerly housed a dairy and has gone through many uses since. There, Sociology shared space with Anthropology, Fine Art, and university activities related to furniture storage, mail delivery, and other less sanitary pursuits. In 1977, the department moved to 203 College Street, where it occupied two floors of rented space in an undistinguished office building above a bank, a copy shop and a Starbucks. Though more hygienic, these quarters were also insufficient. As in the Borden Building, at 203 College Street the Sociology department continued to lack space for student offices, computing facilities, research activities, teaching, and socializing. It remained impossible to build a sense of community in such quarters, as successive reviewers noted.

I took office as Chair in 1997. The problems facing the department were to find suitable space for the department, organize a strong staff, generate a sense of community, and support a strengthened research thrust. There were several opportunities to resolve these challenges. One was a new Dean—a young, former Chair of Geography, Carl Amrhein, who was responsive to the needs of social science departments like ours with a heavy teaching responsibility. Another was a five-year planning window titled "Raising Our Sights," which invited us all to think more creatively: to create new programs and hire particularly accomplished and promising young scholars to replace an aging faculty that was starting to retire. A third was a shift in the research focus of funding agencies away from pure research toward applied research, especially research that was policy-focused on topics such as health. A fourth was the support and encouragement of Wellesley Central Health Corporation, headed by our colleague Dennis Magill.

Indications of what followed can be demonstrated with a few figures. They describe some of the changes in our department between 1997 and 2003, and in some respects depict what happened during my Chairmanship. The amount of research grant dollars administered in the department in-

725 Spadina Avenue: Department of Sociology 2000-Present
PHOTO: STEPHEN CAULFIELD

creased from $125,922 in 1997 to $2,253,373 in 2001-2002. During the same period, undergraduate courses increased from thirty-eight to forty-one, and the number of students registered grew dramatically from 3,701 to 4,848. These numbers show that we have been able to maintain our commitment to excellence in teaching. Indeed, seven faculty members have won the prestigious Faculty of Arts and Science Outstanding Teaching Award: Bernd Baldus, Dean Behrens, Dennis W. Magill, Lorne Tepperman, Jack Veugelers, Sandy Welsh, and Irving Zeitlin. New faculty members on the St. George Campus are Brent Berry, Monica Boyd, Joseph Bryant, John Myles, Ito Peng, and Judith Taylor.

HOW WE DEALT WITH THESE PROBLEMS: KEY ACCOMPLISHMENTS

In the last six years, we have maintained a high level of teaching activity while producing continued levels of high quality research. Important changes include new funding, new staff positions, and the recruitment of new staff members. New funding came from some private sources, including the one million dollar gift of an endowed chair in honour of S.D. Clark, the founder of the department. The most immediately visible change, however, was the move to our new location.

Department of Sociology Staff, 2003: (Back row, left to right): Jeannette Wright, Tina Colomvakos, Tanya Jewell, Linda L. Gardiner; (Front row, left to right): Anne Shipley, Anne Mitchell, Don Bai, Maymie Howe

In 2000, following a period of extensive planning and consultation about the department's space needs, the department moved to its present location. The department today occupies two and a half renovated floors of the western wing of the Faculty of Education Building at the corner of Spadina Avenue and Bloor Street. The new quarters provide, among other things, offices for all faculty and all doctoral students still in residence, a study room for Master's students, two seminar rooms, administrative offices, research project space, three computing laboratories, a multimedia classroom, and shared offices for West and East campus colleagues and sessional faculty. These new facilities are much used and make possible new synergies. They have also increased pride, interaction, collegiality, and productivity.

Equally important was the improvement in our staff complement. At the beginning of my term, there were four staff members; today there are seven and a half. All of these staff members have played a critical role in helping the department to carry out its research and teaching functions, and to budget faculty time and money most effectively. I greatly appreciate all of their contributions. Of the current staff, only one—Jeannette Wright, a veteran of thirty years' magnificent service to the department—remains from 1997.

As I noted above, research funds in the department have increased over the period, thanks largely to the efforts of Research Officer Linn Clark. Linn has been instrumental in boosting the total number of grant applications by faculty members and the proportion that are successful, thus helping to bring many more research dollars into the department. In March 2003, eight faculty members received SSHRC awards valued at $1,374,007. In addition, faculty are co-investigators on projects funded by external granting agencies at a level of more than three million dollars. This significant increase in research activity has been achieved at the same time as undergraduate enrolments have risen significantly, signalling a great achievement by our faculty, with Linn's able assistance.

Over a dozen new faculty positions were funded and filled in the last six years. Some were senior positions, most importantly four endowed chairs: specifically, the privately endowed S.D. Clark Chair (held by William Michelson), two Canada Research Chairs (held by John Myles and Monica Boyd), and the Harney Chair in Ethnic, Immigration, and Pluralism Studies (held by Jeffrey Reitz).

The planning and implementation of new facilities, new staff, and new faculty has gone hand in hand with the cultivation of a new openness in the department. There is now more faculty involvement in decision making, via faculty meetings and participation on a variety of new or reconstituted committees. These include the Executive Committee, Gender Committee, Space Committee, and Computing Committee, as well as older, more established committees such as the Graduate and Undergraduate Curriculum Committees. This change has helped to improve relations with our graduate students, who serve on some of these committees. A more equal distribution of teaching responsibilities has also helped to improve the civic culture.

We also enjoy new rituals in the department. These include the annual S.D. Clark Lecture, organized largely by Chairholder William Michelson. To date, Anthony Giddens, Lloyd Axworthy, and Charles Tilly have presented the lecture. A reception, a dinner, and other events accompany the event. Additionally, we have been building our alumni relations. In particular, Linda Gardiner has been active preparing the alumni newsletter, and planning annual student awards events, and other alumni/faculty/student get-togethers. Another new initiative in the alumni area is a job shadowing and mentorship program, which pairs appropriate alumni with Sociology undergraduate students. This is a program that was initiated by the Undergraduate Sociology Students Union and is ably supervised by Anne Mitchell, Undergraduate Advisor, and Linda Gardiner.

A major new teaching initiative in the last five years has been the Health Studies Program, developed in collaboration with University College and Public Health Science (Faculty of Medicine). Under the directorship of Dennis Magill, this Program has admitted its first cohort of high-quality

John Hannigan (Associate Chair, Graduate Affairs), Dennis W. Magill (Associate Chair, Undergraduate Affairs), Charles Jones (Associate Chair, Graduate Affairs), Lorne Tepperman (Chair)

undergraduate students. Related to this is a strong new emphasis on research in the health area. The department is ready, when the time is ripe, to develop a new Social Policy Program in conjunction with Trinity College, Political Science, and other departments. We have already made a great appointment in that area—Ito Peng—as the junior position attached to the S.D. Clark Chair.

Efforts have been made, both within the department and across the university, to rationalize the relations between the St. George campus and the two suburban campuses. Important new faculty recruitment is continuing on the suburban campuses and, increasingly, appointments that are being made by the increasingly autonomous "departments" at Scarborough and Mississauga will shape our graduate faculty.

As a department, we have continued to foster links with Asia—specifically, with Viet Nam, China, Taiwan, Japan, and Korea—through collaborative research projects, visiting scholars on both sides, and increasingly, admissions of graduate students from these countries. Our new colleague, Ito Peng, has already been named a Fellow of the Asian Institute at the Munk Centre for International Studies.

All of these changes have relied on strong administrative support. Throughout my term of office, I have co-chaired the department with my

Associate Chairs. Chief among them was Dennis Magill, who has long served as Associate Chair for Undergraduate Studies, and for one year, served as Acting Chair while I was on leave. Dennis has been a continued, indispensable source of support and wise advice. In 2003, in recognition of his contribution, the Department established the Dennis William Magill Award, which will be awarded annually to the graduating Sociology major or specialist with the highest average in Sociology undergraduate courses. John Hannigan and Charles Jones have excellently filled the role of Associate Chair for Graduate Studies during my Chairmanship. Additionally, I am grateful to a number of colleagues, many who served on the Executive Committee, for their effort and dedication to the department's needs.

DID THE ISSUES AND PROBLEMS CHANGE OVER TIME?

As one might expect, the issues and problems our department faced changed over time. As we solved old problems, such as the space and staffing issues, new problems came to the fore.

Chief among these were budgetary problems, which throughout the 1990s we had hoped would be temporary. Unfortunately, they turned out to be more permanent features of current provincial government-university relations. Every year of my Chairmanship has brought new uncertainties and crises over funding, and along with this, new challenges regarding ways of positioning the department to meet these problems. It has become clear that although we are expected to take a leading role in sociological research within the university, Canada, and North America, we are also expected to teach increasing numbers of undergraduate students. Undergraduate students, in effect, pay the university's bills, though undergraduate teaching is far from our most prestigious activity within the university.

This flood of undergraduates has been fed by four factors in particular: the so-called *double cohort*—a result of program changes in the Ontario secondary schools; a continued rise in participation in higher education by Canada's young people; a growing demand for education at the University of Toronto; and, as noted, the continued need to raise university revenues through increasing tuition and adding ever larger numbers of undergraduate students. Currently, our department is struggling to find ways to deal with the competing demands of large-scale, high-quality undergraduate education and large-scale, high-quality sociological research.

Another new challenge is the "raising of our sights," driven not by new budgetary opportunities, but by new administrative officers and policies. A new President, brought in from MIT, and a new Provost, brought in from Michigan, have made clear that our standards of hiring, tenure, productivity, and promotion will all be monitored and enforced more rigorously than ever before.

Currently, we face the task of planning to specialize in a smaller number of sociological areas. Reaching a consensus on our areas of specialization, and other related issues, will not be easy. Like other Sociology departments, we comprise a variety of independent-minded scholars and researchers. We come from a variety of intellectual backgrounds, and pursue varied goals in teaching and research. Naturally, we want to see our own particular visions of sociology prevail in the coming re-organization. Yet, we will have to find ways of identifying our strengths and pursuing our long-term institutional interests.

Along the way, we will have to re-organize the graduate program to reflect new institutional demands for specialization and focus. Historically, we have admitted a wide variety of students and provided them with a range of courses and research opportunities. Implementation of the new university-wide graduate funding package has made it necessary to streamline our graduate program—reducing time to completion of graduate degrees—and recruit students more vigorously in areas where our department is most research-active. In future, more student funding will come from research grants. This, in turn, may mean that more grants will be needed to support the graduate program; faculty researchers with more funds will have a larger responsibility and right to recruit students; and excellent students with interests that do not articulate well with the department's research activities may have to be turned away.

CHANGE AND CIVILITY

Institutional change is never easy, especially when it threatens to downgrade people's areas of interest. Then, difficult choices often strain collegiality and community in the department.

The attempt to establish "community" in the department has succeeded in many respects, but in other respects we still have a long way to go. There is a natural conflict between the ideal of community on the one hand and individual achievement on the other. We all want to belong to a community of people who will help us achieve our goals. This need is critically important for our graduate students, but no less important for mature scholars (though often less evident).

At the same time, from childhood on we are all urged and trained to pursue the highest standards of scholarship in our teaching and research. We learn these goals as students and teach them to our own students, and these goals are constantly reinforced in the peer-review processes associated with publication and grantsmanship. The pursuit of individual achievement is difficult and often lonely. It demands sacrifice and engenders pride. Sometimes, however, it produces a sense of superiority and exclusivity among those who succeed most. It then becomes easy to lose a spirit of collegiality and to imagine that we can succeed alone, through personal efforts individually pursued.

This tension between individual and collective efforts—and the accompanying tension over rewards—is built into the structure of any university and will never disappear. Yet, we must continue, as other departments have done, to strive for collegiality and *civility*. Civility, a defining Canadian trait, is much undervalued in a highly competitive world. Yet, we cannot survive and improve as a department without this universal lubricant of collegiality.

My period as Chair has seen some outbreaks of shameful, aggressive incivility, and on those occasions, we have found out that we are extremely vulnerable. The university, for all its bureaucratic rules, has a soft cultural underbelly and often cannot defend itself against incivility. The reasons are simple enough: it—we—stand for freedom of speech. The university is nothing if it is not a place where colleagues and students can and should express very different views about fundamental social, political, and ethical issues. Moreover, we recognize the strains under which many of our students and faculty operate, and these strains may give rise to outbursts of intemperance and incivility.

So, often we have to suffer incivility in silence, yet we register the injuries and they affect our lives together. More work will be needed to remedy this problem. Perhaps a new Chair or different processes of governance will make additional headway on this issue.

OUR PLACE IN CANADIAN SOCIOLOGY

Our department has always had a special place in Canadian sociology. We cannot claim that all the important work has been done here in Toronto, or that all the work done in our department has been important. Yet, historically, we have written many of the fundamental books and articles, carried out the key sociological projects, and trained the leading sociological researchers of tomorrow. We continue to do these things today.

As Chair, I found myself in a position of conflict vis-à-vis other departments of Sociology. We are in competition with other departments across Canada, and beyond: in competition for the best students, the best faculty members, and the best grants. Yet, we are also the colleagues of sociologists in Montreal, Edmonton, Vancouver, and elsewhere. We need to act, often, in a concerted fashion to protect and promote the image and interests of Sociology as a discipline in Canada and the world. Currently, we lack a good institutional framework for doing so. Our national institutions, such as the Canadian Sociology and Anthropology Association, the *Canadian Review of Sociology and Anthropology*, and the *Canadian Journal of Sociology*, are too weak and fragmented to do this, though in recent years we have seen an improvement in the leadership of these institutions.

I tried for three years to remedy this problem by convening and leading the Committee of Chairs of Ontario Sociology Departments. This activity helped me to see that many of our problems—for example, underfunding—are common to all Ontario Sociology departments, and that many others—for example, the lack of job guidance and job placement for our first-degree graduates—are probably common to Sociology departments everywhere. There are no easy and quick fixes to these problems. Yet, I believe that our department can still play a key leadership role. Comparatively, we are the biggest, most productive, and best-resourced department of Sociology in Canada.

As I complete my tour of duty as Chair, we face as many challenges as we did before; however, they are new problems with a higher level of complexity. In a sense, the stakes are also higher. We are poised to compete in a larger arena, as per the expectations of our President and Provost. I leave the office of Chair confident that we have a faculty, staff, and students who are equal to this challenge.

Lorne Tepperman

Department of Sociology Teaching Staff: 1963-1964 to 2002-2003

1963-1964

Beals, R.C.	Lecturer
Burnet, J.R.	Assistant Professor
Clark, S.D.	Professor, Chair
Giffen, P.J.	Associate Professor
Hall, O.	Professor
James, R.L.	Professor, Visiting
Lucas, R.A.	Lecturer
Pullman, D.R.	Instructor
Reuschemeyer, D.	Assistant Professor
Willmott, D.E.	Assistant Professor
Zakuta, L.	Assistant Professor

1964-1965

Beals, R.C.	Lecturer
Burnet, J.R.	Associate Professor
Clark, S.D.	Professor, Chair
Cooperstock, H.	Special Lecturer
Giffen, P.J.	Associate Professor
Hall, O.	Professor
James, R.L.	Professor
Johnson, W.D.H.	Lecturer
Lobser, J.J.	Assistant Professor
Lucas, R.A.	Lecturer
Marshall, T.H.	Professor, Visiting
Nishio, H.K.	Assistant Professor
Reuschemeyer, D.	Assistant Professor
Willmott, D.E.	Assistant Professor
Zakuta, L.	Associate Professor

1965-1966

Beals, R.C.	Assistant Professor
Burnet, J.R.	Associate Professor
Carlton, R.A.	Lecturer
Clark, S.D.	Professor, Chair
Cooperstock, H.	Assistant Professor
Currie, I.D.	Lecturer
Giffen, P.J.	Associate Professor
Hall, O.	Professor
James, R.L.	Professor
Johnson, W.D.H.	Lecturer
Lobser, J.J.	Assistant Professor
Lucas, R.A.	Assistant Professor
Maxwell, T.R.	Special Lecturer
Nishio, H.K.	Assistant Professor
Reuschemeyer, D.	Associate Professor
Scott, M.B.	Lecturer
Tilly, C.	Professor
Walker, K.N.	Assistant Professor
Willmott, D.E.	Associate Professor
Zakuta, L.	Associate Professor

1966-1967

Beals, R.C.	Assistant Professor
Burnet, J.R.	Associate Professor
Carlton, R.A.	Lecturer
Clark, S.D.	Professor, Chair
Cook, S.	Instructor
Cooper, M.	Instructor
Cooperstock, H.	Assistant Professor
Currie, I.D.	Lecturer
Feuer, L.S.	Professor
Francis, E.K.	Professor, Visiting
Giffen, P.J.	Professor
Hall, O.	Professor
James, R.L.	Professor
Johnson, W.D.H.	Lecturer
Lobser, J.J.	Associate Professor, Associate Chair
Lucas, R.A.	Assistant Professor
Michelson, W.M.	Assistant Professor
Nishio, H.K.	Associate Professor
Tilly, C.	Professor
Walker, K.N.	Assistant Professor
Weinberg, I.	Assistant Professor
Willmott, D.E.	Associate Professor
Zakuta, L.	Associate Professor

1967-1968

Baum, R.C.	Assistant Professor
Beals, R.C.	Assistant Professor
Bell, N.W.	Professor
Carlton, R.A.	Assistant Professor
Clark, S.D.	Professor, Chair
Cook, S.	Instructor
Cooper, M.	Lecturer
Cooperstock, H.	Assistant Professor
Currie, I.D.	Lecturer
Feuer, L.S.	Professor
Francis, E.K.	Professor, Visiting
Gerson, W.M.	Associate Professor
Giffen, P.J.	Professor
Hall, O.	Professor
Hanna, M.E.	Lecturer
Harvey, E.B.	Assistant Professor
James, R.L.	Professor
Kelner, M.J.	Lecturer
Lennards, J.L.	Assistant Professor
Lobser, J.J.	Associate Professor, Associate Chair
Lucas, R.A.	Associate Professor
Michelson, W.M.	Assistant Professor
Nishio, H.K.	Associate Professor
Powell, A.T.R.	Lecturer
Tilly, C.	Professor
Walker, K.N.	Assistant Professor
Weinberg, I.	Assistant Professor
Wellman, B.	Assistant Professor
Zakuta, L.	Associate Professor

1968-1969

Badgley, R.F.	Associate Professor
Baum, R.C.	Assistant Professor
Beals, R.C.	Assistant Professor
Bell, N.W.	Professor
Bennett, A.	Lecturer
Breton, R.	Associate Professor
Carlton, R.A.	Assistant Professor
Clark, S.D.	Professor, Chair
Cooper, M.	Lecturer
Cooperstock, H.	Assistant Professor
Currie, I.D.	Assistant Professor
Feuer, L.S.	Professor
Gerson, W.M.	Associate Professor
Giffen, P.J.	Professor
Hall, O.	Professor
Hanna, M.E.	Lecturer
Harvey, E.B.	Assistant Professor
James, R.L.	Professor
Joyner, J.	Instructor
Kelner, M.J.	Lecturer
Kemper, T.D.	Associate Professor
Lennards, J.L.	Assistant Professor
Lobser, J.J.	Associate Professor
Lucas, R.A.	Associate Professor
Michelson, W.M.	Associate Professor
Nishio, H.K.	Associate Professor
Porter, J.	Professor
Powell, A.T.R.	Lecturer
Tilly, C.	Professor
Walker, K.N.	Assistant Professor
Wayne, J.	Lecturer
Weeks, P.	Instructor
Weinberg, I. (obit)	Associate Professor
Wellman, B.	Assistant Professor
Zakuta, L.	Professor

1969-1970

Badgley, R.F.	Associate Professor
Baldus, B.	Special Lecturer
Beals, R.C.	Assistant Professor
Bell, N.W.	Professor
Bennett, A.	Lecturer
Blishen, B.	Professor, Visiting
Breton, R.	Associate Professor
Burnside, R.W.	Lecturer
Clark, S.D.	Professor
Cook, S.	Lecturer
Cooper, M.	Lecturer
Cooperstock, H.	Associate Professor
Currie, I.D.	Assistant Professor
Feuer, L.S.	Professor
Gerson, W.M.	Associate Professor
Giffen, P.J.	Professor, Chair
Hall, O.	Professor
Hanna, M.E.	Lecturer
Harvey, E.B.	Associate Professor
James, R.L.	Professor
Joyner, J.	Lecturer
Kalbach, W.	Professor
Kelner, M.J.	Assistant Professor
Kemper, T.D.	Associate Professor
Lee, J.A.	Assistant Professor
Lennards, J.L.	Assistant Professor
Lobser, J.J.	Associate Professor
Lucas, R.A.	Associate Professor
Makler, H.M.	Assistant Professor
Michelson, W.M.	Associate Professor
Nishio, H.K.	Associate Professor
O'Toole, R.	Lecturer
Phillips, W.	Assistant Professor
Powell, A.T.R.	Lecturer
Tepperman, L.	Assistant Professor
Walker, K.N.	Assistant Professor

Wayne, J.	Lecturer
Wellman, B.	Assistant Professor
Wilkins, J.	Associate Professor
Zakuta, L.	Professor

1970-1971

Badgley, R.F.	Associate Professor
Baldus, B.	Assistant Professor
Beals, R.C.	Assistant Professor
Bell, N.W.	Professor
Bennett, A.	Assistant Professor
Breslauer, H.J.	Lecturer
Breton, R.	Associate Professor
Burnside, R.W.	Lecturer
Clark, S.D.	Professor
Cook, S.	Lecturer
Cooper, M.	Lecturer
Cooperstock, H.	Associate Professor
Currie, I.D.	Assistant Professor
Feuer, L.S.	Professor
Gerson, W.M.	Associate Professor
Giffen, P.J.	Professor, Chair
Hall, O.	Professor
Hanna, M.E.	Assistant Professor
Harvey, E.B.	Associate Professor
Howard, L.	Assistant Professor
Isajiw, W.W.	Associate Professor
James, R.L.	Professor
Joyner, J.	Lecturer
Kalbach, W.	Professor
Kelner, M.J.	Assistant Professor
Lee, J.A.	Assistant Professor
Lennards, J.L.	Assistant Professor
Lobser, J.J.	Associate Professor
Lorion, P.	Assistant Professor
Lucas, R.A.	Associate Professor
Magill, D.W.	Assistant Professor
Makler, H.M.	Assistant Professor
Michelson, W.M.	Associate Professor
Nishio, H.K.	Associate Professor
O'Toole, R.	Lecturer
Phillips, W.	Assistant Professor

Powell, A.T.R.	Lecturer
Reitz, J.G.	Assistant Professor
Salaff, J.W.	Assistant Professor
Simpson, J.H.	Assistant Professor
Smith, A.H.	Assistant Professor
Solomon, P.H.	Assistant Professor
Tepperman, L.	Assistant Professor
Turk, J.L.	Assistant Professor
Walker, K.N.	Associate Professor
Wayne, J.	Lecturer
Wellman, B.	Assistant Professor
Wilkins, J.	Associate Professor
Zakuta, L.	Professor

1971-1972

Badgley, R.F.	Professor
Baldus, B.	Assistant Professor
Beals, R.C.	Assistant Professor
Bell, N.W.	Professor
Bennett, A.	Assistant Professor
Breslauer, H.J.	Assistant Professor
Breton, R.	Professor
Burnside, R.W. (obit.)	Lecturer
Clark, S.D.	Professor
Cook, S.	Lecturer
Cooper, M.	Lecturer
Cooperstock, H.	Associate Professor
Currie, I.D.	Assistant Professor
Feuer, L.S.	Professor
Gerson, W.M.	Associate Professor
Giffen, P.J.	Professor, Chair
Hall, O.	Professor
Hanna, M.E.	Assistant Professor
Harvey, E.B.	Associate Professor
Howard, L.	Assistant Professor
Isajiw, W.W.	Associate Professor
James, R.L.	Professor
Joyner, J.	Lecturer
Kalbach, W.	Professor
Kelner, M.J.	Assistant Professor
Kervin, J.B.	Assistant Professor
Lee, J.A.	Assistant Professor
Lennards, J.L.	Assistant Professor
Lorion, P.	Assistant Professor
Lucas, R.A.	Professor
Magill, D.W.	Assistant Professor
Makler, H.M.	Assistant Professor
Michelson, W.M.	Associate Professor
New, P.K.	Professor
Nishio, H.K.	Professor
O'Toole, R.	Lecturer

Phillips, W.	Assistant Professor
Powell, A.T.R.	Lecturer
Reitz, J.G.	Assistant Professor
Rosen, R.	Lecturer
Salaff, J.W.	Assistant Professor
Simpson, J.H.	Assistant Professor
Smith, A.H.	Assistant Professor
Solomon, P.H.	Assistant Professor
Tepperman, L.	Assistant Professor
Turk, J.L.	Assistant Professor
Walker, K.N.	Associate Professor
Wayne, J.	Assistant Professor
Wellman, B.	Assistant Professor
Wilkins, J.	Associate Professor
Zakuta, L.	Professor

1972-1973

Badgley, R.F.	Professor
Baldus, B.	Assistant Professor
Beals, R.C.	Assistant Professor
Bell, N.W.	Professor
Bennett, A.	Assistant Professor
Breslauer, H.J.	Assistant Professor
Breton, R.	Professor
Burnside, R.W.	Lecturer
Clark, S.D.	Professor
Cook, S.	Lecturer
Cooperstock, H.	Associate Professor
Currie, I.D.	Assistant Professor
Felt, L.F.	Assistant Professor
Feuer, L.S.	Professor
Gerson, W.M.	Associate Professor
Giffen, P.J.	Professor
Hall, O.	Professor
Hartmann, N.	Lecturer
Harvey, E.B.	Associate Professor
Howard, L.	Assistant Professor
Isajiw, W.W.	Associate Professor
James, R.L.	Professor
Johnson, L.	Assistant Professor, Visiting
Joyner, J.	Lecturer
Kalbach, W.	Professor
Kelner, M.J.	Assistant Professor
Kervin, J.B.	Assistant Professor
Lee, J.A.	Assistant Professor
Lennards, J.L.	Assistant Professor
Lorion, P.	Assistant Professor
Lucas, R.A.	Professor
Magill, D.W.	Assistant Professor
Makler, H.M.	Assistant Professor
Marsden, L.R.	Assistant Professor, Visiting
Michelson, W.M.	Professor
New, P.K.	Professor

Nishio, H.K.	Professor
Osborn, R.W.	Associate Professor
O'Toole, R.	Lecturer
Phillips, W.	Assistant Professor
Powell, A.T.R.	Lecturer
Reitz, J.G.	Assistant Professor
Salaff, J.W.	Assistant Professor
Simpson, J.H.	Assistant Professor
Smith, A.H.	Assistant Professor
Solomon, P.H.	Assistant Professor
Spencer, M.W.	Assistant Professor
Tepperman, L.	Assistant Professor
Tirl, J.	Assistant Professor
Walker, K.N.	Associate Professor
Wayne, J.	Assistant Professor
Wellman, B.	Associate Professor
Wilkins, J.	Associate Professor
Zakuta, L.	Professor
Zeitlin, I.M.	Professor, Chair

1973-1974

Badgley, R.F.	Professor
Baldus, B.	Assistant Professor
Beals, R.C.	Assistant Professor
Bell, N.W.	Professor
Bennett, A.	Assistant Professor
Berkowitz, S.D.	Lecturer
Breslauer, H.J.	Assistant Professor
Breton, R.	Professor
Clark, S.D.	Professor
Cooperstock, H.	Associate Professor
Currie, I.D.	Assistant Professor
Erickson, B.	Assistant Professor
Felt, L.F.	Assistant Professor
Feuer, L.S.	Professor
Giffen, P.J.	Professor
Hall, O.	Professor
Hartmann, N.	Lecturer
Harvey, E.B.	Associate Professor
Heap, J.	Lecturer
Howard, L.	Assistant Professor
Howell, N.L.	Associate Professor
Isajiw, W.W.	Associate Professor
James, R.L.	Professor
Johnson, L.	Assistant Professor
Joyner, J.	Lecturer
Kalbach, W.	Professor
Kelner, M.J.	Assistant Professor
Kervin, J.B.	Assistant Professor
Lee, J.A.	Assistant Professor
Lennards, J.L.	Assistant Professor
Lorion, P.	Assistant Professor
Lucas, R.A.	Professor
MacKay, R.W.	Lecturer
Magill, D.W.	Assistant Professor
Makler, H.M.	Assistant Professor
Marsden, L.R.	Assistant Professor

Michelson, W.M.	Professor
New, P.K.	Professor
Nishio, H.K.	Professor
Osborn, R.W.	Associate Professor
O'Toole, R.	Assistant Professor
Phillips, W.	Assistant Professor
Powell, A.T.R.	Assistant Professor
Reitz, J.G.	Assistant Professor
Salaff, J.W.	Assistant Professor
Simpson, J.H.	Assistant Professor
Small, S.	Assistant Professor
Smith, A.H.	Assistant Professor
Solomon, P.H.	Assistant Professor
Spencer, M.W.	Assistant Professor
Tepperman, L.	Associate Professor
Tsurumi, K.	Professor, Visiting
Turk, J.L.	Assistant Professor
Walker, K.N.	Associate Professor
Wayne, J.	Assistant Professor
Wellman, B.	Associate Professor
Wilkins, J.	Associate Professor
Zakuta, L.	Professor
Zeitlin, I.M.	Professor, Chair

1974-1975

Badgley, R.F.	Professor
Baldus, B.	Assistant Professor
Beals, R.C.	Assistant Professor
Bell, N.W.	Professor
Bennett, A.	Assistant Professor
Berkowitz, S.D.	Lecturer
Bodemann, Y.M.	Lecturer
Boughey, H.	Associate Professor
Breslauer, H.J.	Assistant Professor
Breton, R.	Professor
Clark, S.D.	Professor
Cooperstock, H.	Associate Professor
Erickson, B.	Assistant Professor
Feuer, L.S.	Professor
Giffen, P.J.	Professor
Hagan, J.	Assistant Professor
Hall, O.	Professor
Harvey, E.B.	Professor
Heap, J.	Lecturer
Howard, L.	Assistant Professor
Howell, N.L.	Associate Professor
Isajiw, W.W.	Associate Professor
James, R.L.	Professor
Kalbach, W.	Professor
Kelner, M.J.	Assistant Professor
Kervin, J.B.	Assistant Professor
Lee, J.A.	Assistant Professor
Lorion, P.	Assistant Professor
Lucas, R.A.	Professor
MacKay, R.W.	Assistant Professor
Magill, D.W.	Associate Professor
Makler, H.M.	Assistant Professor
Marsden, L.R.	Assistant Professor
Michelson, W.M.	Professor
New, P.K.	Professor
Nishio, H.K.	Professor

Orbach, H.	Professor, Visiting
Osborn, R.W.	Associate Professor
O'Toole, R.	Assistant Professor
Piccone, P.	Professor, Visiting
Powell, A.T.R.	Assistant Professor
Reitz, J.G.	Assistant Professor
Rex, J.	Professor
Roman, R.	Associate Professor
Salaff, J.W.	Assistant Professor
Silva, E.	Associate Professor
Simpson, J.H.	Assistant Professor
Small, S.	Assistant Professor
Solomon, P.H.	Assistant Professor
Spencer, M.W.	Assistant Professor
Tepperman, L.	Associate Professor
Tirl, J.	Assistant Professor
Turk, A.T.	Professor
Walker, K.N.	Associate Professor
Wayne, J.	Assistant Professor
Wellman, B.	Associate Professor
Wilkins, J.	Associate Professor
Zakuta, L.	Professor, Visiting
Zeitlin, I.M.	Professor, Chair

1975-1976

Badgley, R.F.	Professor
Baldus, B.	Assistant Professor
Baum, G.G.	Professor
Beals, R.C.	Associate Professor
Bell, N.W.	Professor
Berkowitz, S.D.	Assistant Professor
Bodemann, Y.M.	Lecturer
Boughey, H.	Associate Professor
Breslauer, H.J.	Assistant Professor
Breton, R.	Professor
Campbell, D.F.	Associate Professor, Visiting
Clark, S.D.	Professor
Cooperstock, H.	Associate Professor
Erickson, B.	Assistant Professor
Ericson, R.V.	Assistant Professor
Feuer, L.S.	Professor
Giffen, P.J.	Professor
Hagan, J.	Assistant Professor
Hall, O.	Professor Emeritus
Harvey, E.B.	Professor
Howard, L.	Assistant Professor
Howell, N.L.	Associate Professor
Isajiw, W.W.	Associate Professor
James, R.L.	Professor
Kalbach, W.	Professor
Kelner, M.J.	Assistant Professor
Kervin, J.B.	Assistant Professor
Lee, J.A.	Associate Professor
Leiss, W.	Associate Professor
Lorion, P.	Assistant Professor
Lucas, R.A.	Professor
MacKay, R.W.	Assistant Professor
Magill, D.W.	Associate Professor, Associate Chair
Makler, H.M.	Assistant Professor
Marsden, L.R.	Assistant Professor
Michelson, W.M.	Professor

Murmis, M.	Professor, Visiting
New, P.K.	Professor
Nishio, H.K.	Professor
Osborn, R.W.	Associate Professor
O'Toole, R.	Associate Professor
Powell, A.T.R.	Assistant Professor
Reitz, J.G.	Associate Professor
Roman, R.	Associate Professor
Salaff, J.W.	Associate Professor
Silva, E.	Associate Professor
Simpson, J.H.	Assistant Professor
Small, S.	Assistant Professor
Smith, D.	Associate Professor, Visiting
Solomon, P.H.	Assistant Professor
Spencer, M.W.	Assistant Professor
Tepperman, L.	Associate Professor
Turk, A.T.	Professor
Turk, J.L.	Assistant Professor
Walker, K.N.	Associate Professor
Wayne, J.	Assistant Professor
Wellman, B.	Associate Professor
Wilkins, J.	Associate Professor
Zakuta, L.	Professor
Zeitlin, I.M.	Professor, Chair

1976-1977

Badgley, R.F.	Professor
Baldus, B.	Associate Professor
Beals, R.C.	Associate Professor
Bell, N.W.	Professor
Berkowitz, S.D.	Assistant Professor
Bodemann, Y.M.	Lecturer
Boughey, H.	Associate Professor
Breslauer, H.J.	Assistant Professor
Breton, R.	Professor
Campbell, D.F.	Associate Professor, Visiting
Clark, S.D.	Professor Emeritus
Cooperstock, H.	Associate Professor
de Lannoy, J.L.	Assistant Professor
Erickson, B.	Associate Professor
Ericson, R.V.	Assistant Professor
Giffen, P.J.	Professor
Green, B.S.	Assistant Professor
Hagan, J.	Assistant Professor
Hall, O.	Professor Emeritus
Harvey, E.B.	Professor
Howell, N.L.	Associate Professor
Isajiw, W.W.	Associate Professor
James, R.L.	Professor
Kalbach, W.	Professor
Kelner, M.J.	Assistant Professor
Kervin, J.B.	Associate Professor
Lee, J.A.	Associate Professor
Lorion, P.	Assistant Professor
Lucas, R.A.	Professor
MacKay, R.W.	Assistant Professor
Magill, D.W.	Associate Professor, Associate Chair
Makler, H.M.	Associate Professor
Marsden, L.R.	Associate Professor
Michelson, W.M.	Professor
Murmis, M.	Professor, Visiting
New, P.K.	Professor

Nishio, H.K.	Professor
Osborn, R.W.	Associate Professor
O'Toole, R.	Associate Professor
Powell, A.T.R.	Assistant Professor
Reitz, J.G.	Associate Professor
Roman, R.	Associate Professor
Salaff, J.W.	Associate Professor
Silva, E.	Associate Professor
Simpson, J.H.	Associate Professor
Small, S.	Assistant Professor
Spencer, M.W.	Associate Professor
Tepperman, L.	Associate Professor
Tirl, J.	Associate Professor
Turk, A.T.	Professor
Walker, K.N.	Associate Professor
Wayne, J.	Associate Professor
Wellman, B.	Associate Professor
Wilkins, J.	Associate Professor
Zakuta, L.	Professor
Zeitlin, I.M.	Professor, Chair

1977-1978

Badgley, R.F.	Professor
Baldus, B.	Associate Professor
Beals, R.C.	Associate Professor
Bell, N.W.	Professor
Berkowitz, S.D.	Assistant Professor
Bodemann, Y.M.	Assistant Professor
Boughey, H.	Associate Professor
Breton, R.	Professor
Campbell, D.F.	Associate Professor
Clark, S.D.	Professor Emeritus
Cooperstock, H.	Associate Professor
de Lannoy, J.L.	Associate Professor
Erickson, B.	Associate Professor
Ericson, R.V.	Assistant Professor
Friedmann, H.	Assistant Professor
Giffen, P.J.	Professor
Hagan, J.	Associate Professor
Hall, O.	Professor Emeritus
Hammond, M.	Assistant Professor
Harvey, E.B.	Professor
Howell, N.L.	Associate Professor
Isajiw, W.W.	Associate Professor
James, R.L.	Professor
Kalbach, W.	Professor
Kervin, J.B.	Associate Professor
Lee, J.A.	Associate Professor
Lorion, P.	Assistant Professor
Lucas, R.A.	Professor
MacKay, R.W.	Assistant Professor
Magill, D.W.	Associate Professor
Makler, H.M.	Associate Professor
Marsden, L.R.	Associate Professor, Chair
Michelson, W.M.	Professor
Murmis, M.	Associate Professor
New, P.K.	Professor
Nishio, H.K.	Professor

Osborn, R.W.	Associate Professor
O'Toole, R.	Associate Professor
Powell, A.T.R.	Assistant Professor
Reitz, J.G.	Associate Professor
Roman, R.	Associate Professor
Salaff, J.W.	Associate Professor
Silva, E.	Associate Professor
Simpson, J.H.	Associate Professor
Small, S.	Assistant Professor
Spencer, M.W.	Associate Professor
Tepperman, L.	Associate Professor
Turk, A.T.	Professor
Turk, J.L.	Associate Professor
Ungar, S.	Assistant Professor
Wagner, D.	Lecturer
Walker, K.N.	Associate Professor
Wayne, J.	Associate Professor
Wellman, B.	Associate Professor
Wilkins, J.	Associate Professor
Zakuta, L.	Professor
Zeitlin, I.M.	Professor

1978-1979

Badgley, R.F.	Professor
Baldus, B.	Associate Professor
Beals, R.C.	Associate Professor
Bell, N.W.	Professor
Berkowitz, S.D.	Assistant Professor
Bodemann, Y.M.	Assistant Professor
Boughey, H.	Associate Professor
Breton, R.	Professor
Brym, R.	Assistant Professor
Campbell, D.F.	Associate Professor
Clark, S.D.	Professor Emeritus
Cooperstock, H.	Associate Professor
de Lannoy, J.L.	Associate Professor
Erickson, B.	Associate Professor
Ericson, R.V.	Assistant Professor
Friedmann, H.	Assistant Professor
Giffen, P.J.	Professor
Hagan, J.	Associate Professor
Hall, O.	Professor Emeritus
Hammond, M.	Assistant Professor
Hannigan, J.	Assistant Professor
Harvey, E.B.	Professor
Howell, N.L.	Associate Professor
Isajiw, W.W.	Professor
James, R.L.	Professor
Kalbach, W.	Professor
Kervin, J.B.	Associate Professor
Lee, J.A.	Associate Professor
Lucas, R.A. (obit)	Professor
MacKay, R.W.	Associate Professor
Magill, D.W.	Associate Professor
Makler, H.M.	Associate Professor
Marsden, L.R.	Associate Professor, Chair
Michelson, W.M.	Professor
Murmis, M.	Associate Professor
New, P.K.	Professor

Nishio, H.K.	Professor
Osborn, R.W.	Associate Professor
O'Toole, R.	Associate Professor
Reitz, J.G.	Associate Professor
Roman, R.	Associate Professor
Salaff, J.W.	Associate Professor
Silva, E.	Associate Professor
Simpson, J.H.	Associate Professor
Spencer, M.W.	Associate Professor
Tepperman, L.	Professor
Turk, A.T.	Professor
Turk, J.L.	Associate Professor
Ungar, S.	Assistant Professor
Walker, K.N.	Associate Professor
Wayne, J.	Associate Professor
Wellman, B.	Associate Professor
Wilkins, J.	Associate Professor
Zakuta, L.	Professor
Zeitlin, I.M.	Professor

1979-1980

Badgley, R.F.	Professor
Baldus, B.	Associate Professor
Baum, G.G.	Professor
Beals, R.C.	Associate Professor
Bell, N.W.	Professor
Berkowitz, S.D.	Assistant Professor
Bodemann, Y.M.	Assistant Professor
Boughey, H.	Associate Professor
Breton, R.	Professor
Brym, R.	Assistant Professor
Campbell, D.F.	Associate Professor
Clark, S.D.	Professor Emeritus
Cooperstock, H.	Associate Professor
de Lannoy, J.L.	Associate Professor
Duffy, A.D.	Assistant Professor
Erickson, B.	Associate Professor
Ericson, R.V.	Associate Professor
Friedmann, H.	Assistant Professor
Giffen, P.J.	Professor
Gillis, A.R.	Associate Professor
Hagan, J.	Associate Professor
Hall, O.	Professor Emeritus
Hammond, M.	Assistant Professor
Hannigan, J.	Assistant Professor
Harvey, E.B.	Professor
Howell, N.L.	Professor, Acting Chair
Isajiw, W.W.	Professor
James, R.L.	Professor
Kalbach, W.	Professor
Kelner, M.J.	Associate Professor
Kervin, J.B.	Associate Professor
Lee, J.A.	Associate Professor
MacKay, R.W.	Associate Professor
Magill, D.W.	Associate Professor
Makler, H.M.	Associate Professor
Marsden, L.R.	Professor

Michelson, W.M.	Professor
Murmis, M.	Associate Professor
New, P.K.	Professor
Nishio, H.K.	Professor
Osborn, R.W.	Associate Professor
O'Toole, R.	Associate Professor
Reitz, J.G.	Associate Professor
Roman, R.	Associate Professor
Salaff, J.W.	Associate Professor
Silva, E.	Associate Professor
Simpson, J.H.	Associate Professor
Spencer, M.W.	Associate Professor
Stein, A.	Associate Professor
Tepperman, L.	Professor
Tirl, J.	Associate Professor
Turk, A.T.	Professor
Ungar, S.	Assistant Professor
Walker, K.N.	Associate Professor
Wayne, J.	Associate Professor
Wellman, B.	Associate Professor
Wilkins, J.	Associate Professor
Zakuta, L.	Professor
Zeitlin, I.M.	Professor

1980-1981

Badgley, R.F.	Professor
Baldus, B.	Associate Professor, Associate Chair
Baum, G.G.	Professor
Beals, R.C.	Associate Professor
Bell, N.W.	Professor
Berkowitz, S.D.	Assistant Professor
Bodemann, Y.M.	Associate Professor
Boughey, H.	Associate Professor
Breton, R.	Professor
Brym, R.	Associate Professor
Campbell, D.F.	Associate Professor
Clark, S.D.	Professor Emeritus
Cooperstock, H.	Associate Professor
de Lannoy, J.L.	Associate Professor
Duffy, A.D.	Assistant Professor
Erickson, B.	Associate Professor
Ericson, R.V.	Associate Professor
Friedmann, H.	Assistant Professor
Giffen, P.J.	Professor
Gillis, A.R.	Associate Professor
Hagan, J.	Professor
Hall, O.	Professor Emeritus
Hammond, M.	Assistant Professor
Hannigan, J.	Assistant Professor
Harvey, E.B.	Professor
Howell, N.L.	Professor
Isajiw, W.W.	Professor
James, R.L.	Professor
Kalbach, W.	Professor
Kelner, M.J.	Associate Professor
Kervin, J.B.	Associate Professor
Lee, J.A.	Associate Professor
MacKay, R.W.	Associate Professor
Magill, D.W.	Associate Professor
Makler, H.M.	Associate Professor
Marsden, L.R.	Professor

Michelson, W.M.	Professor
Murmis, M.	Associate Professor
New, P.K.	Professor
Nishio, H.K.	Professor
O'Toole, R.	Associate Professor
Reitz, J.G.	Professor, Chair
Roman, R.	Associate Professor
Salaff, J.W.	Associate Professor
Silva, E.	Associate Professor
Simpson, J.H.	Associate Professor
Spencer, M.W.	Associate Professor
Stein, A.	Associate Professor
Tepperman, L.	Professor
Turk, A.T.	Professor
Turk, J.L.	Associate Professor
Ungar, S.	Assistant Professor
Walker, K.N.	Associate Professor
Wayne, J.	Associate Professor
Wellman, B.	Professor
Wilkins, J.	Associate Professor
Zakuta, L.	Professor
Zeitlin, I.M.	Professor

1981-1982

Badgley, R.F.	Professor
Baldus, B.	Associate Professor, Associate Chair
Baum, G.G.	Professor
Beals, R.C.	Associate Professor
Bell, N.W.	Professor
Bodemann, Y.M.	Associate Professor
Boughey, H.	Associate Professor
Breton, R.	Professor
Brym, R.	Associate Professor
Campbell, D.F.	Associate Professor
Clark, S.D.	Professor Emeritus
Cooperstock, H.	Associate Professor
de Lannoy, J.L.	Associate Professor
Duffy, A.D.	Assistant Professor
Erickson, B.	Associate Professor
Ericson, R.V.	Associate Professor
Friedmann, H.	Associate Professor
Giffen, P.J.	Professor
Gillis, A.R.	Associate Professor
Hagan, J.	Professor
Hall, O.	Professor Emeritus
Hammond, M.	Assistant Professor
Hannigan, J.	Assistant Professor
Harvey, E.B.	Professor
Howell, N.L.	Professor
Isajiw, W.W.	Professor
James, R.L.	Professor
Kalbach, W.	Professor
Kelner, M.J.	Professor
Kervin, J.B.	Associate Professor
Lee, J.A.	Associate Professor
MacKay, R.W.	Associate Professor
Magill, D.W.	Associate Professor
Makler, H.M.	Associate Professor
Marsden, L.R.	Professor
Michelson, W.M.	Professor

Murmis, M.	Associate Professor
New, P.K.	Professor
Nishio, H.K.	Professor
O'Toole, R.	Associate Professor
Reitz, J.G.	Professor, Chair
Roman, R.	Associate Professor
Salaff, J.W.	Associate Professor
Silva, E.	Associate Professor
Simpson, J.H.	Associate Professor
Spencer, M.W.	Associate Professor
Stein, A.	Associate Professor
Tepperman, L.	Professor
Turk, A.T.	Professor
Turk, J.L.	Associate Professor
Ungar, S.	Associate Professor
Vanderburg, W.H.	Assistant Professor
Walker, K.N.	Associate Professor
Wayne, J.	Associate Professor
Wellman, B.	Professor
Wilkins, J.	Associate Professor
Zakuta, L.	Professor
Zeitlin, I.M.	Professor

1982-1983

Badgley, R.F.	Professor
Baldus, B.	Associate Professor, Associate Chair
Baum, G.G.	Professor
Beals, R.C.	Associate Professor
Bell, N.W.	Professor
Bodemann, Y.M.	Associate Professor
Boughey, H.	Associate Professor
Breton, R.	Professor
Brym, R.	Associate Professor
Campbell, D.F.	Associate Professor
Clark, S.D.	Professor Emeritus
Cooperstock, H.	Associate Professor
de Lannoy, J.L.	Associate Professor
Duffy, A.D.	Assistant Professor
Erickson, B.	Associate Professor
Ericson, R.V.	Professor
Friedmann, H.	Associate Professor
Giffen, P.J.	Professor
Gillis, A.R.	Associate Professor
Hagan, J.	Professor
Hall, O.	Professor Emeritus
Hammond, M.	Assistant Professor
Hannigan, J.	Assistant Professor
Harvey, E.B.	Professor
Howell, N.L.	Professor
Isajiw, W.W.	Professor
James, R.L.	Professor
Jones, C.L.	Assistant Professor
Kalbach, W.	Professor
Kelner, M.J.	Professor
Kervin, J.B.	Associate Professor
Lee, J.A.	Associate Professor
MacKay, R.W.	Associate Professor
Magill, D.W.	Associate Professor
Makler, H.M.	Associate Professor
Marsden, L.R.	Professor

Michelson, W.M.	Professor
Murmis, M.	Associate Professor
New, P.K.	Professor
Nishio, H.K.	Professor
O'Toole, R.	Associate Professor
Reitz, J.G.	Professor, Chair
Roman, R.	Associate Professor
Salaff, J.W.	Professor
Silva, E.	Associate Professor
Simpson, J.H.	Associate Professor
Spencer, M.W.	Associate Professor
Stein, A.	Associate Professor
Tepperman, L.	Professor
Turk, A.T.	Professor
Turk, J.L.	Associate Professor
Ungar, S.	Associate Professor
Vanderburg, W.H.	Assistant Professor
Walker, K.N.	Associate Professor
Wayne, J.	Associate Professor
Wellman, B.	Professor
Wilkins, J.	Associate Professor
Zakuta, L.	Professor
Zeitlin, I.M.	Professor

1983-1984

Badgley, R.F.	Professor
Baldus, B.	Associate Professor, Associate Chair
Baum, G.G.	Professor
Beals, R.C.	Associate Professor
Bell, N.W.	Professor
Bodemann, Y.M.	Associate Professor
Boughey, H.	Associate Professor
Breton, R.	Professor
Brym, R.	Associate Professor
Campbell, D.F.	Associate Professor
Clark, S.D.	Professor Emeritus
Cooperstock, H.	Associate Professor
de Lannoy, J.L.	Associate Professor
Duffy, A.D.	Assistant Professor
Erickson, B.	Associate Professor
Ericson, R.V.	Professor
Friedmann, H.	Associate Professor
Giffen, P.J.	Professor
Gillis, A.R.	Associate Professor
Hagan, J.	Professor
Hall, O.	Professor Emeritus
Hammond, M.	Associate Professor
Hannigan, J.	Associate Professor
Harvey, E.B.	Professor
Howell, N.L.	Professor
Isajiw, W.W.	Professor
James, R.L.	Professor
Jones, C.L.	Professor
Kalbach, W.	Professor
Kelner, M.J.	Professor
Kervin, J.B.	Associate Professor
Lee, J.A.	Associate Professor
MacKay, R.W.	Associate Professor
Magill, D.W.	Associate Professor
Makler, H.M.	Associate Professor
Marsden, L.R.	Professor

Michelson, W.M.	Professor
Murmis, M.	Associate Professor
Nishio, H.K.	Professor
O'Toole, R.	Associate Professor
Reitz, J.G.	Professor, Chair
Roman, R.	Associate Professor
Salaff, J.W.	Professor
Silva, E.	Associate Professor
Simpson, J.H.	Associate Professor
Spencer, M.W.	Associate Professor
Stein, A.	Associate Professor
Tepperman, L.	Professor
Turk, A.T.	Professor
Turk, J.L.	Associate Professor
Ungar, S.	Associate Professor
Vanderburg, W.H.	Assistant Professor
Walker, K.N.	Associate Professor
Wayne, J.	Associate Professor
Wellman, B.	Professor
Zakuta, L.	Professor
Zeitlin, I.M.	Professor

1984-1985

Badgley, R.F.	Professor
Baldus, B.	Associate Professor, Associate Chair
Baum, G.G.	Professor
Beals, R.C.	Associate Professor
Bell, N.W.	Professor
Blute, M.	Assistant Professor
Bodemann, Y.M.	Associate Professor
Boughey, H.	Associate Professor
Breton, R.	Professor
Brym, R.	Associate Professor
Campbell, D.F.	Associate Professor
Clark, S.D.	Professor Emeritus
de Lannoy, J.L.	Associate Professor
Duffy, A.D.	Assistant Professor
Erickson, B.	Associate Professor
Ericson, R.V.	Professor
Friedmann, H.	Associate Professor
Giffen, P.J.	Professor
Gillis, A.R.	Associate Professor
Hagan, J.	Professor
Hall, O.	Professor Emeritus
Hammond, M.	Associate Professor
Hannigan, J.	Associate Professor
Harvey, E.B.	Professor
Howell, N.L.	Professor
Isajiw, W.W.	Professor
James, R.L.	Professor
Jones, C.L.	Professor
Kalbach, W.	Professor
Kelner, M.J.	Professor
Kervin, J.B.	Associate Professor
Lee, J.A.	Associate Professor
MacKay, R.W.	Associate Professor
Magill, D.W.	Associate Professor
Makler, H.M.	Associate Professor
Marsden, L.R.	Professor

Michelson, W.M.	Professor
Murmis, M.	Associate Professor
Nishio, H.K.	Professor
O'Toole, R.	Associate Professor
Pupo, N.	Assistant Professor
Reitz, J.G.	Professor, Chair
Roman, R.	Associate Professor
Salaff, J.W.	Professor
Silva, E.	Associate Professor
Simpson, J.H.	Associate Professor
Spencer, M.W.	Associate Professor
Stein, A.	Associate Professor
Tepperman, L.	Professor
Turk, A.T.	Professor
Turk, J.L.	Associate Professor
Ungar, S.	Associate Professor
Vanderburg, W.H.	Assistant Professor
Wayne, J.	Associate Professor
Wellman, B.	Professor
Zakuta, L.	Professor
Zeitlin, I.M.	Professor

1985-1986

Badgley, R.F.	Professor
Baldus, B.	Associate Professor
Baum, G.G.	Professor
Beals, R.C.	Associate Professor
Bell, N.W.	Professor
Blute, M.	Associate Professor
Bodemann, Y.M.	Associate Professor
Boughey, H.	Associate Professor
Breton, R.	Professor
Brym, R.	Professor
Campbell, D.F.	Associate Professor
Clark, S.D.	Professor Emeritus
de Lannoy, J.L.	Associate Professor
Erickson, B.	Professor
Ericson, R.V.	Professor
Fox, B.	Assistant Professor
Friedmann, H.	Associate Professor
Giffen, P.J.	Professor Emeritus
Gillis, A.R.	Professor
Green, B.S.	Assistant Professor
Hagan, J.	Professor, Associate Chair
Hall, O.	Professor Emeritus
Hammond, M.	Associate Professor
Hannigan, J.	Associate Professor
Harvey, E.B.	Professor
Howell, N.L.	Professor
Isajiw, W.W.	Professor
James, R.L.	Professor
Jones, C.L.	Professor
Kalbach, W.	Professor
Kelner, M.J.	Professor
Kervin, J.B.	Associate Professor
Lee, J.A.	Associate Professor
MacKay, R.W.	Associate Professor
Magill, D.W.	Associate Professor
Makler, H.M.	Associate Professor

Marsden, L.R.	Professor
Michelson, W.M.	Professor
Milner, C.S.	Assistant Professor
Murmis, M.	Associate Professor
Nishio, H.K.	Professor
O'Toole, R.	Professor
Pupo, N.	Assistant Professor
Reitz, J.G.	Professor
Roman, R.	Associate Professor
Salaff, J.W.	Professor
Silva, E.	Associate Professor
Simpson, J.H.	Associate Professor, Chair
Spencer, M.W.	Associate Professor
Stein, A.	Associate Professor
Tepperman, L.	Professor
Turk, A.T.	Professor
Turk, J.L.	Associate Professor
Ungar, S.	Associate Professor
Vanderburg, W.H.	Assistant Professor
Wayne, J.	Associate Professor
Wellman, B.	Professor
Zeitlin, I.M.	Professor

1986-1987

Badgley, R.F.	Professor
Baldus, B.	Associate Professor
Beals, R.C.	Associate Professor
Bell, N.W.	Professor
Blute, M.	Associate Professor
Bodemann, Y.M.	Associate Professor
Boughey, H.	Associate Professor
Breton, R.	Professor
Brym, R.	Professor
Campbell, D.F.	Associate Professor
Clark, S.D.	Professor Emeritus
de Lannoy, J.L.	Associate Professor
Erickson, B.	Professor
Ericson, R.V.	Professor
Fox, B.	Assistant Professor
Friedmann, H.	Associate Professor
Giffen, P.J.	Professor Emeritus
Gillis, A.R.	Professor
Green, B.S.	Assistant Professor
Hagan, J.	Professor, Associate Chair
Hall, O.	Professor Emeritus
Hammond, M.	Associate Professor
Hannigan, J.	Associate Professor
Harvey, E.B.	Professor
Howell, N.L.	Professor
Isajiw, W.W.	Professor
James, R.L.	Professor
Jones, C.L.	Professor
Kalbach, W.	Professor
Kelner, M.J.	Professor
Kervin, J.B.	Associate Professor
Lee, J.A.	Associate Professor
MacKay, R.W.	Associate Professor
Magill, D.W.	Associate Professor
Makler, H.M.	Associate Professor
Marsden, L.R.	Professor

Michelson, W.M.	Professor
Milner, C.S.	Assistant Professor
Murmis, M.	Associate Professor
Nishio, H.K.	Professor
O'Toole, R.	Professor
Pupo, N.	Assistant Professor
Reitz, J.G.	Professor
Roman, R.	Associate Professor
Salaff, J.W.	Professor
Silva, E.	Associate Professor
Simpson, J.H.	Professor, Chair
Spencer, M.W.	Associate Professor
Stein, A.	Associate Professor
Tepperman, L.	Professor
Turk, A.T.	Professor
Turk, J.L.	Associate Professor
Ungar, S.	Associate Professor
Vanderburg, W.H.	Assistant Professor
Wayne, J.	Associate Professor
Wellman, B.	Professor
Zakuta, L.	Professor Emeritus
Zeitlin, I.M.	Professor

1987-1988

Badgley, R.F.	Professor
Baldus, B.	Associate Professor
Beals, R.C.	Associate Professor
Bell, N.W.	Professor
Blute, M.	Associate Professor
Bodemann, Y.M.	Associate Professor
Boughey, H.	Associate Professor
Breton, R.	Professor
Brym, R.	Professor
Campbell, D.F.	Associate Professor
Clark, S.D.	Professor Emeritus
de Lannoy, J.L.	Associate Professor
Erickson, B.	Professor
Ericson, R.V.	Professor
Fox, B.	Assistant Professor
Friedmann, H.	Associate Professor
Giffen, P.J.	Professor Emeritus
Gillis, A.R.	Professor
Green, B.S.	Assistant Professor
Hagan, J.	Professor
Hall, O.	Professor Emeritus
Hammond, M.	Associate Professor, Associate Chair
Hannigan, J.	Associate Professor
Harvey, E.B.	Professor
Howell, N.L.	Professor
Isajiw, W.W.	Professor
James, R.L.	Professor
Jones, C.L.	Professor
Kalbach, W.	Professor
Kelner, M.J.	Professor
Kervin, J.B.	Associate Professor
Lee, J.A.	Associate Professor
MacKay, R.W.	Associate Professor
Magill, D.W.	Associate Professor
Makler, H.M.	Associate Professor
Marsden, L.R.	Professor

Michelson, W.M.	Professor
Milner, C.S.	Assistant Professor
Murmis, M.	Associate Professor
Nishio, H.K.	Professor
O'Toole, R.	Professor
Pupo, N.	Assistant Professor
Reitz, J.G.	Professor
Roman, R.	Associate Professor
Salaff, J.W.	Professor
Silva, E.	Professor
Simpson, J.H.	Professor, Chair
Spencer, M.W.	Associate Professor
Stein, A.	Associate Professor
Tepperman, L.	Professor
Turk, A.T.	Professor, Associate Chair
Turk, J.L.	Associate Professor
Ungar, S.	Associate Professor
Vanderburg, W.H.	Assistant Professor
Wayne, J.	Associate Professor
Wellman, B.	Professor
Zakuta, L.	Professor Emeritus
Zeitlin, I.M.	Professor

1988-1989

Badgley, R.F.	Professor
Baldus, B.	Associate Professor
Beals, R.C.	Associate Professor
Bell, N.W.	Professor
Blute, M.	Associate Professor
Bodemann, Y.M.	Associate Professor
Boughey, H.	Associate Professor
Breton, R.	Professor
Brym, R.	Professor
Campbell, D.F.	Associate Professor
Clark, S.D.	Professor Emeritus
de Lannoy, J.L.	Associate Professor
Erickson, B.	Professor
Ericson, R.V.	Professor
Fox, B.	Assistant Professor
Friedmann, H.	Associate Professor
Giffen, P.J.	Professor Emeritus
Gillis, A.R.	Professor
Green, B.S.	Assistant Professor
Hagan, J.	Professor
Hall, O.	Professor Emeritus
Hammond, M.	Associate Professor, Associate Chair
Hannigan, J.	Associate Professor
Harvey, E.B.	Professor
Howell, N.L.	Professor
Isajiw, W.W.	Professor
James, R.L.	Professor
Jones, C.L.	Professor
Kalbach, W.	Professor
Kelner, M.J.	Professor
Kervin, J.B.	Associate Professor
Lee, J.A.	Associate Professor
MacKay, R.W.	Associate Professor
Magill, D.W.	Associate Professor
Makler, H.M.	Associate Professor
Marsden, L.R.	Professor

Michelson, W.M.	Professor
Milner, C.S.	Assistant Professor
Murmis, M.	Associate Professor
Nishio, H.K.	Professor
O'Toole, R.	Professor
Pupo, N.	Assistant Professor
Reitz, J.G.	Professor
Roman, R.	Associate Professor
Salaff, J.W.	Professor
Silva, E.	Professor
Simpson, J.H.	Professor, Chair
Spencer, M.W.	Associate Professor
Stein, A.	Associate Professor
Tepperman, L.	Professor
Turk, A.T.	Professor, Associate Chair
Turk, J.L.	Associate Professor
Ungar, S.	Associate Professor
Vanderburg, W.H.	Assistant Professor
Wayne, J.	Associate Professor
Wellman, B.	Professor
Zakuta, L.	Professor Emeritus
Zeitlin, I.M.	Professor

1989-1990

Badgley, R.F.	Professor
Baldus, B.	Associate Professor
Beals, R.C.	Associate Professor
Bell, N.W.	Professor
Blute, M.	Associate Professor
Bodemann, Y.M.	Associate Professor
Boughey, H.	Associate Professor
Breton, R.	Professor
Brownfield, D.	Assistant Professor
Brym, R.	Professor
Campbell, D.F.	Associate Professor
Clark, S.D.	Professor Emeritus
de Lannoy, J.L.	Associate Professor
Erickson, B.	Professor
Ericson, R.V.	Professor
Fox, B.	Assistant Professor
Friedmann, H.	Associate Professor
Gartner, R.	Assistant Professor
Giffen, P.J.	Professor Emeritus
Gillis, A.R.	Professor
Hagan, J.	Professor
Hall, O.	Professor Emeritus
Hammond, M.	Associate Professor
Hannigan, J.	Associate Professor
Harvey, E.B.	Professor
Howell, N.L.	Professor
Isajiw, W.W.	Professor
James, R.L.	Professor
Jones, C.L.	Professor, Associate Chair
Kalbach, W.	Professor
Kelner, M.J.	Professor
Kervin, J.B.	Associate Professor
Lee, J.A.	Associate Professor
MacKay, R.W.	Associate Professor
Magill, D.W.	Associate Professor, Associate Chair
Makler, H.M.	Associate Professor

Marsden, L.R.	Professor
Michelson, W.M.	Professor
Nishio, H.K.	Professor
O'Toole, R.	Professor
Reitz, J.G.	Professor
Roman, R.	Associate Professor
Salaff, J.W.	Professor
Silva, E.	Professor
Simpson, J.H.	Professor, Chair
Spencer, M.W.	Associate Professor
Stein, A.	Associate Professor
Tanner, J.	Assistant Professor
Tepperman, L.	Professor
Turk, A.T.	Professor
Turk, J.L.	Associate Professor
Tuzlak, A.	Assistant Professor
Ungar, S.	Associate Professor
Vanderburg, W.H.	Associate Professor
Wayne, J.	Associate Professor
Wellman, B.	Professor
Wheaton, B.	Associate Professor
Zakuta, L.	Professor Emeritus
Zeitlin, I.M.	Professor

1990-1991

Badgley, R.F.	Professor
Baldus, B.	Associate Professor
Beals, R.C.	Associate Professor
Bell, N.W.	Professor
Blute, M.	Associate Professor
Bodemann, Y.M.	Associate Professor
Boughey, H.	Associate Professor
Breton, R.	Professor
Brownfield, D.	Associate Professor
Brym, R.	Professor
Campbell, D.F.	Associate Professor
Clark, S.D.	Professor Emeritus
de Lannoy, J.L.	Associate Professor
Erickson, B.	Professor
Ericson, R.V.	Professor
Fox, B.	Associate Professor
Friedmann, H.	Professor
Gartner, R.	Associate Professor
Giffen, P.J.	Professor Emeritus
Gillis, A.R.	Professor
Hagan, J.	Professor
Hall, O.	Professor Emeritus
Hammond, M.	Associate Professor
Hannigan, J.	Associate Professor
Harvey, E.B.	Professor
Howell, N.L.	Professor
Isajiw, W.W.	Professor
James, R.L.	Professor
Jones, C.L.	Professor, Associate Chair
Kalbach, W.	Professor
Kelner, M.J.	Professor
Kervin, J.B.	Associate Professor
Lee, J.A.	Associate Professor
MacKay, R.W.	Associate Professor
Magill, D.W.	Associate Professor, Associate Chair
Makler, H.M.	Associate Professor

Marsden, L.R.	Professor
Michelson, W.M.	Professor
Nishio, H.K.	Professor
O'Toole, R.	Professor
Reitz, J.G.	Professor
Roman, R.	Associate Professor
Salaff, J.W.	Professor
Silva, E.	Professor
Simpson, J.H.	Professor, Chair
Spencer, M.W.	Associate Professor
Stein, A.	Associate Professor
Tanner, J.	Assistant Professor
Tepperman, L.	Professor
Turk, A.T.	Professor
Turk, J.L.	Associate Professor
Turner, R.J.	Professor
Tuzlak, A.	Assistant Professor
Ungar, S.	Associate Professor
Vanderburg, W.H.	Associate Professor
Wayne, J.	Associate Professor
Wellman, B.	Professor
Wheaton, B.	Associate Professor
Zakuta, L.	Professor Emeritus
Zeitlin, I.M.	Professor

1991-1992

Badgley, R.F.	Professor
Baldus, B.	Professor
Beals, R.C.	Associate Professor
Bell, N.W.	Professor
Blute, M.	Associate Professor
Bodemann, Y.M.	Associate Professor
Boughey, H.	Associate Professor
Breton, R.	Professor
Brownfield, D.	Associate Professor
Brym, R.	Professor
Campbell, D.F.	Associate Professor
Clark, S.D.	Professor Emeritus
de Lannoy, J.L.	Associate Professor
Erickson, B.	Professor
Ericson, R.V.	Professor
Fox, B.	Associate Professor
Friedmann, H.	Professor
Gartner, R.	Associate Professor
Giffen, P.J.	Professor Emeritus
Gillis, A.R.	Professor
Green, B.S.	Senior Tutor
Hagan, J.	Professor
Hall, O.	Professor Emeritus
Hammond, M.	Associate Professor
Hannigan, J.	Associate Professor
Harvey, E.B.	Professor
Howell, N.L.	Professor
Isajiw, W.W.	Professor
James, R.L.	Professor
Jones, C.L.	Professor, Associate Chair
Kalbach, W.	Professor Emeritus
Kelner, M.J.	Professor
Kervin, J.B.	Associate Professor
Lee, J.A.	Associate Professor
MacKay, R.W.	Associate Professor
Magill, D.W.	Associate Professor, Associate Chair

Makler, H.M.	Associate Professor
Marsden, L.R.	Professor
Michelson, W.M.	Professor
Nishio, H.K.	Professor Emeritus
O'Toole, R.	Professor
Reitz, J.G.	Professor
Roman, R.	Associate Professor
Salaff, J.W.	Professor
Silva, E.	Professor
Simpson, J.H.	Professor, Chair
Sorenson, A.M.	Assistant Professor
Spencer, M.W.	Associate Professor
Stein, A.	Associate Professor
Tanner, J.	Associate Professor
Tepperman, L.	Professor
Turner, R.J.	Professor
Tuzlak, A.	Assistant Professor
Ungar, S.	Associate Professor
Vanderburg, W.H.	Associate Professor
Wayne, J.	Associate Professor
Wellman, B.	Professor
Wheaton, B.	Associate Professor
Zakuta, L.	Professor Emeritus
Zeitlin, I.M.	Professor

1992-1993

Badgley, R.F.	Professor
Baldus, B.	Professor
Beals, R.C.	Associate Professor
Bell, N.W.	Professor
Blute, M.	Associate Professor
Bodemann, Y.M.	Associate Professor
Boughey, H.	Associate Professor
Breton, R.	Professor
Brownfield, D.	Associate Professor
Brym, R.	Professor
Campbell, D.F.	Associate Professor
Clark, S.D.	Professor Emeritus
de Lannoy, J.L.	Associate Professor
Erickson, B.	Professor
Ericson, R.V.	Professor
Fox, B.	Associate Professor
Friedmann, H.	Professor
Gartner, R.	Associate Professor
Giffen, P.J.	Professor Emeritus
Gillis, A.R.	Professor
Green, B.S.	Senior Tutor
Hagan, J.	Professor
Hall, O.	Professor Emeritus
Hammond, M.	Associate Professor
Hannigan, J.	Associate Professor
Harvey, E.B.	Professor
Howell, N.L.	Professor
Hsiung, P.C.	Assistant Professor
Isajiw, W.W.	Professor
James, R.L.	Professor
Jones, C.L.	Professor, Associate Chair
Kalbach, W.	Professor Emeritus
Kelner, M.J.	Professor
Kervin, J.B.	Associate Professor
Lee, J.A.	Associate Professor
MacKay, R.W.	Associate Professor

Magill, D.W.	Professor, Associate Chair
Makler, H.M.	Associate Professor
Marsden, L.R.	Professor
Michelson, W.M.	Professor
Nishio, H.K.	Professor Emeritus
O'Toole, R.	Professor
Reitz, J.G.	Professor
Roman, R.	Associate Professor
Salaff, J.W.	Professor
Silva, E.	Professor
Simpson, J.H.	Professor, Chair
Sorenson, A.M.	Assistant Professor
Spencer, M.W.	Associate Professor
Stein, A.	Associate Professor
Tanner, J.	Associate Professor
Tepperman, L.	Professor
Turner, R.J.	Professor
Tuzlak, A.	Assistant Professor
Ungar, S.	Associate Professor
Vanderburg, W.H.	Associate Professor
Wayne, J.	Associate Professor
Wellman, B.	Professor
Wheaton, B.	Professor
Zakuta, L.	Professor Emeritus
Zeitlin, I.M.	Professor

1993-1994

Badgley, R.F.	Professor
Baldus, B.	Professor
Bell, N.W.	Professor
Blute, M.	Associate Professor
Bodemann, Y.M.	Associate Professor
Boughey, H.	Associate Professor
Breton, R.	Professor Emeritus
Brownfield, D.	Associate Professor
Brym, R.	Professor
Campbell, D.F.	Associate Professor
Clark, S.D.	Professor Emeritus
de Lannoy, J.L.	Associate Professor
Erickson, B.	Professor
Erickson, P.G.	Adjunct Professor
Ericson, R.V.	Professor
Fox, B.	Associate Professor
Friedmann, H.	Professor
Gartner, R.	Associate Professor
Giffen, P.J.	Professor Emeritus
Gillis, A.R.	Professor
Green, B.S.	Senior Tutor
Hagan, J.	Professor
Hall, O.	Professor Emeritus
Hammond, M.	Associate Professor
Hannigan, J.	Associate Professor
Harvey, E.B.	Professor
Howell, N.L.	Professor
Hsiung, P.C.	Assistant Professor
Isajiw, W.W.	Professor
James, R.L.	Professor Emeritus
Jones, C.L.	Professor, Associate Chair
Kalbach, W.	Professor Emeritus
Kelner, M.J.	Professor
Kervin, J.B.	Associate Professor
Layton, J.	Adjunct Associate Professor
Lee, J.A.	Associate Professor

MacKay, R.W.	Associate Professor
Magill, D.W.	Professor, Associate Chair
Michelson, W.M.	Professor
Nishio, H.K.	Professor Emeritus
O'Toole, R.	Professor
Reitz, J.G.	Professor
Roman, R.	Associate Professor
Salaff, J.W.	Professor
Silva, E.	Professor
Simpson, J.H.	Professor, Chair
Sorenson, A.M.	Assistant Professor
Spencer, M.W.	Associate Professor
Stein, A.	Associate Professor
Tanner, J.	Associate Professor
Tepperman, L.	Professor
Turner, R.J.	Professor
Tuzlak, A.	Associate Professor
Ungar, S.	Associate Professor
Vanderburg, W.H.	Associate Professor
Wayne, J.	Associate Professor
Wellman, B.	Professor
Wheaton, B.	Professor
Zakuta, L.	Professor Emeritus
Zeitlin, I.M.	Professor

1994-1995

Badgley, R.F.	Professor
Baldus, B.	Professor
Bell, N.W. (obit)	Professor Emeritus
Blute, M.	Associate Professor
Bodemann, Y.M.	Associate Professor
Boughey, H.	Associate Professor
Breton, R.	Professor Emeritus
Brownfield, D.	Associate Professor
Brym, R.	Professor
Campbell, D.F.	Associate Professor
Clark, S.D.	Professor Emeritus
de Lannoy, J.L.	Associate Professor
Erickson, B.	Professor
Erickson, P.G.	Adjunct Professor
Fong, W.C.	Assistant Professor
Fox, B.	Associate Professor
Friedmann, H.	Professor
Gartner, R.	Professor
Giffen, P.J.	Professor Emeritus
Gillis, A.R.	Professor
Green, B.S.	Senior Tutor
Hagan, J.	Professor
Hall, O.	Professor Emeritus
Hammond, M.	Associate Professor
Hannigan, J.	Associate Professor
Harvey, E.B.	Professor
Howell, N.L.	Professor
Hsiung, P.C.	Assistant Professor
Isajiw, W.W.	Professor
James, R.L.	Professor Emeritus
Jones, C.L.	Professor, Associate Chair
Kalbach, W.	Professor Emeritus
Kelner, M.J.	Professor Emeritus
Kervin, J.B.	Professor
Layton, J.	Adjunct Associate Professor
Lee, J.A.	Associate Professor

Magill, D.W.	Professor, Associate Chair
Michelson, W.M.	Professor
Nishio, H.K.	Professor Emeritus
O'Toole, R.	Professor
Reitz, J.G.	Professor
Roman, R.	Associate Professor
Salaff, J.W.	Professor
Sev'er, A.	Associate Professor
Silva, E.	Professor
Simpson, J.H.	Professor, Chair
Sorenson, A.M.	Associate Professor
Spencer, M.W.	Associate Professor
Stein, A.	Associate Professor
Tanner, J.	Associate Professor
Tepperman, L.	Professor
Turner, R.J.	Professor
Ungar, S.	Associate Professor
Vanderburg, W.H.	Associate Professor
Wayne, J.	Associate Professor
Wellman, B.	Professor
Wheaton, B.	Professor
Zakuta, L.	Professor Emeritus
Zeitlin, I.M.	Professor

1995-1996

Badgley, R.F.	Professor
Baldus, B.	Professor
Blute, M.	Associate Professor
Bodemann, Y.M.	Professor
Boughey, H.	Associate Professor
Breton, R.	Professor Emeritus
Brownfield, D.	Associate Professor
Brym, R.	Professor
Campbell, D.F.	Associate Professor
Clark, S.D.	Professor Emeritus
de Lannoy, J.L.	Associate Professor
Erickson, B.	Professor
Erickson, P.G.	Adjunct Professor
Fong, W.C.	Assistant Professor
Fox, B.	Associate Professor
Friedmann, H.	Professor
Gartner, R.	Professor
Giffen, P.J.	Professor Emeritus
Gillis, A.R.	Professor
Green, B.S.	Senior Tutor
Hagan, J.	Professor
Hall, O.	Professor Emeritus
Hammond, M.	Associate Professor
Hannigan, J.	Associate Professor
Harvey, E.B.	Professor
Howell, N.L.	Professor
Hsiung, P.C.	Assistant Professor
Isajiw, W.W.	Professor
James, R.L.	Professor Emeritus
Jones, C.L.	Professor, Associate Chair
Kalbach, W.	Professor Emeritus
Kelner, M.J.	Professor Emeritus
Kervin, J.B.	Professor
Layton, J.	Adjunct Associate Professor
Lee, J.A.	Associate Professor
MacKay, R.W.	Associate Professor

Magill, D.W.	Professor, Associate Chair
Michelson, W.M.	Professor
Nishio, H.K.	Professor Emeritus
O'Toole, R.	Professor
Reitz, J.G.	Professor
Roman, R.	Associate Professor
Salaff, J.W.	Professor
Sev'er, A.	Associate Professor
Silva, E.	Professor
Simpson, J.H.	Professor, Chair
Sorenson, A.M.	Associate Professor
Spencer, M.W.	Associate Professor
Stein, A.	Associate Professor
Tanner, J.	Associate Professor
Tepperman, L.	Professor
Turner, R.J.	Professor
Ungar, S.	Associate Professor
Vanderburg, W.H.	Associate Professor
Wayne, J.	Associate Professor
Wellman, B.	Professor
Welsh, S.	Lecturer
Wheaton, B.	Professor
Zakuta, L.	Professor Emeritus
Zeitlin, I.M.	Professor Emeritus

1996-1997

Badgley, R.F.	Professor
Baldus, B.	Professor
Blute, M.	Associate Professor
Bodemann, Y.M.	Professor
Breton, R.	Professor Emeritus
Brownfield, D.	Associate Professor
Brym, R.	Professor
Campbell, D.F.	Associate Professor
Clark, S.D.	Professor Emeritus
de Lannoy, J.L.	Associate Professor
Erickson, B.	Professor
Erickson, P.G.	Adjunct Professor
Fong, W.C.	Assistant Professor
Fox, B.	Associate Professor
Friedmann, H.	Professor
Gartner, R.	Professor
Giffen, P.J.	Professor Emeritus
Gillis, A.R.	Professor
Green, B.S.	Senior Tutor
Hagan, J.	Professor
Hall, O.	Professor Emeritus
Hammond, M.	Associate Professor
Hannigan, J.	Associate Professor
Harvey, E.B.	Professor
Howell, N.L.	Professor
Hsiung, P.C.	Assistant Professor
Isajiw, W.W.	Professor
James, R.L.	Professor Emeritus
Jones, C.L.	Professor, Associate Chair
Kalbach, W.	Professor Emeritus
Kelner, M.J.	Professor Emeritus
Kervin, J.B.	Professor
Lee, J.A.	Associate Professor
MacKay, R.W.	Associate Professor
Magill, D.W.	Professor, Associate Chair
Makler, H.M.	Professor Emeritus

Michelson, W.M.	Professor
Nishio, H.K.	Professor Emeritus
O'Toole, R.	Professor
Reitz, J.G.	Professor
Roman, R.	Associate Professor
Salaff, J.W.	Professor
Sev'er, A.	Associate Professor
Silva, E.	Professor
Simpson, J.H.	Professor, Chair
Sorenson, A.M.	Associate Professor
Spencer, M.W.	Associate Professor
Stein, A.	Associate Professor
Tanner, J.	Associate Professor
Tepperman, L.	Professor
Ungar, S.	Associate Professor
Vanderburg, W.H.	Associate Professor
Wayne, J.	Associate Professor
Wellman, B.	Professor
Welsh, S.	Assistant Professor
Wheaton, B.	Professor
Zakuta, L.	Professor Emeritus
Zeitlin, I.M.	Professor Emeritus

1997-1998

Badgley, R.F.	Professor
Baldus, B.	Professor
Blute, M.	Associate Professor
Bodemann, Y.M.	Professor
Breton, R.	Professor Emeritus
Brownfield, D.	Associate Professor
Brym, R.	Professor
Campbell, D.F.	Professor
Clark, S.D.	Professor Emeritus
de Lannoy, J.L.	Associate Professor
Erickson, B.	Professor
Erickson, P.G.	Adjunct Professor
Fong, W.C.	Assistant Professor
Fox, B.	Associate Professor
Friedmann, H.	Professor
Gartner, R.	Professor
Giffen, P.J.	Professor Emeritus
Gillis, A.R.	Professor
Green, B.S.	Senior Tutor
Hagan, J.	Professor
Hall, O.	Professor Emeritus
Hammond, M.	Associate Professor
Hannigan, J.	Associate Professor
Harvey, E.B.	Professor
Howell, N.L.	Professor
Hsiung, P.C.	Associate Professor
Isajiw, W.W.	Professor
James, R.L.	Professor Emeritus
Jones, C.L.	Professor, Associate Chair
Kalbach, W.	Professor Emeritus
Kelner, M.J.	Professor Emeritus
Kervin, J.B.	Professor
Lee, J.A.	Associate Professor
MacKay, R.W.	Associate Professor
Magee, W.J.	Assistant Professor
Magill, D.W.	Professor, Associate Chair

Makler, H.M.	Professor Emeritus
Michelson, W.M.	Professor
Nishio, H.K.	Professor Emeritus
O'Toole, R.	Professor
Reitz, J.G.	Professor
Roman, R.	Associate Professor
Salaff, J.W.	Professor
Sev'er, A.	Associate Professor
Silva, E.	Professor
Simpson, J.H.	Professor
Sorenson, A.M.	Associate Professor
Spencer, M.W.	Associate Professor
Stein, A.	Associate Professor
Stevens, G.A.	Associate Professor
Tanner, J.	Associate Professor
Tepperman, L.	Professor, Chair
Ungar, S.	Associate Professor
Vanderburg, W.H.	Associate Professor
Veugelers, J.W.P.	Assistant Professor
Wayne, J.	Associate Professor
Wellman, B.	Professor
Welsh, S.	Assistant Professor
Wheaton, B.	Professor
Zakuta, L.	Professor Emeritus
Zeitlin, I.M.	Professor Emeritus

1998-1999

Badgley, R.F.	Professor
Baldus, B.	Professor
Behrens, D.	Assistant Professor
Blute, M.	Associate Professor
Bodemann, Y.M.	Professor
Breton, R.	Professor Emeritus
Brownfield, D.	Associate Professor
Brym, R.	Professor
Campbell, D.F.	Professor
Clark, S.D.	Professor Emeritus
de Lannoy, J.L.	Associate Professor
Erickson, B.	Professor
Erickson, P.G.	Adjunct Professor
Fong, W.C.	Assistant Professor
Fox, B.	Associate Professor
Friedmann, H.	Professor
Gartner, R.	Professor
Giffen, P.J.	Professor Emeritus
Gillis, A.R.	Professor
Green, B.S.	Senior Tutor
Hagan, J.	Professor
Hall, O.	Professor Emeritus
Hammond, M.	Associate Professor
Hannigan, J.	Associate Professor
Harvey, E.B.	Professor
Howell, N.L.	Professor
Hsiung, P.C.	Associate Professor
Isajiw, W.W.	Professor
James, R.L.	Professor Emeritus
Jones, C.L.	Professor, Associate Chair
Kalbach, W.	Professor Emeritus
Kelner, M.J.	Professor Emeritus
Kervin, J.B.	Professor
Lee, J.A.	Associate Professor
MacKay, R.W.	Associate Professor
Magee, W.J.	Assistant Professor

Magill, D.W.	Professor, Associate Chair
Makler, H.M.	Professor Emeritus
Michelson, W.M.	Professor
Nishio, H.K.	Professor Emeritus
O'Toole, R.	Professor
Peressini, T.	Assistant Professor
Reitz, J.G.	Professor
Roman, R.	Associate Professor
Salaff, J.W.	Professor
Sev'er, A.	Associate Professor
Silva, E.	Professor
Simpson, J.H.	Professor
Sorenson, A.M.	Associate Professor
Spencer, M.W.	Professor Emeritus
Stein, A.	Associate Professor
Stevens, G.A.	Professor
Tanner, J.	Associate Professor
Tepperman, L.	Professor, Chair
Ungar, S.	Associate Professor
Vanderburg, W.H.	Associate Professor
Veugelers, J.W.P.	Assistant Professor
Wayne, J.	Associate Professor
Wellman, B.	Professor
Welsh, S.	Assistant Professor
Wheaton, B.	Professor
Zakuta, L.	Professor Emeritus
Zeitlin, I.M.	Professor Emeritus

1999-2000

Badgley, R.F.	Professor
Baldus, B.	Professor
Behrens, D.	Assistant Professor
Bernard, R.B.	Assistant Professor
Blute, M.	Associate Professor
Bodemann, Y.M.	Professor
Breton, R.	Professor Emeritus
Brownfield, D.	Associate Professor
Brym, R.	Professor
Campbell, D.F.	Professor
Clark, S.D.	Professor Emeritus
de Lannoy, J.L.	Associate Professor
Erickson, B.	Professor
Erickson, P.G.	Adjunct Professor
Fong, W.C.	Associate Professor
Fox, B.	Associate Professor
Friedmann, H.	Professor
Gartner, R.	Professor
Giffen, P.J.	Professor Emeritus
Gillis, A.R.	Professor
Green, B.S.	Senior Tutor
Hagan, J.	Professor
Hall, O.	Professor Emeritus
Hammond, M.	Associate Professor
Hannigan, J.	Associate Professor
Harvey, E.B.	Professor
Howell, N.L.	Professor
Hsiung, P.C.	Associate Professor
Isajiw, W.W.	Professor
James, R.L.	Professor Emeritus
Jones, C.L.	Professor, Associate Chair
Kalbach, W.	Professor Emeritus
Kelner, M.J.	Professor Emeritus
Kervin, J.B.	Professor
Lee, J.A.	Associate Professor
MacKay, R.W.	Associate Professor

Magee, W.J.	Assistant Professor
Magill, D.W.	Professor, Associate Chair
Makler, H.M.	Professor Emeritus
Michelson, W.M.	Professor
Nishio, H.K.	Professor Emeritus
O'Toole, R.	Professor
Peressini, T.	Assistant Professor
Reitz, J.G.	Professor
Roman, R.	Associate Professor
Salaff, J.W.	Professor
Sev'er, A.	Associate Professor
Silva, E.	Professor
Simpson, J.H.	Professor
Sorenson, A.M.	Associate Professor
Spencer, M.W.	Professor Emeritus
Stein, A.	Associate Professor
Stevens, G.A.	Professor
Tanner, J.	Associate Professor
Tepperman, L.	Professor, Chair
Ungar, S.	Associate Professor
Vanderburg, W.H.	Associate Professor
Veugelers, J.W.P.	Assistant Professor
Wayne, J.	Associate Professor
Wellman, B.	Professor
Welsh, S.	Assistant Professor
Wheaton, B.	Professor
Zakuta, L.	Professor Emeritus
Zeitlin, I.M.	Professor Emeritus

2000-2001

Badgley, R.F.	Professor
Baldus, B.	Professor
Behrens, D.	Assistant Professor
Bernard, R.B.	Assistant Professor
Blute, M.	Associate Professor
Bodemann, Y.M.	Professor
Breton, R.	Professor Emeritus
Brownfield, D.	Associate Professor
Brym, R.	Professor
Campbell, D.F.	Professor Emeritus
Clark, S.D.	Professor Emeritus
Erickson, B.	Professor
Fong, W.C.	Associate Professor
Fox, B.	Associate Professor
Friedmann, H.	Professor
Gartner, R.	Professor
Giffen, P.J.	Professor Emeritus
Gillis, A.R.	Professor
Green, B.S.	Senior Lecturer
Hagan, J.	Professor
Hall, O.	Professor Emeritus
Hammond, M.	Associate Professor
Hannah-Moffat, K.	Assistant Professor
Hannigan, J.	Professor, Associate Chair
Harvey, E.B.	Professor
Howell, N.L.	Professor, Associate Chair
Hsiung, P.C.	Associate Professor
Isajiw, W.W.	Professor Emeritus
James, R.L.	Professor Emeritus
Jones, C.L.	Professor
Kalbach, W.	Professor Emeritus
Kelner, M.J.	Professor Emeritus
Kervin, J.B.	Professor
MacKay, R.W.	Associate Professor
Magee, W.J.	Assistant Professor
Magill, D.W.	Professor

Makler, H.M.	Professor Emeritus
Michelson, W.M.	Professor
Nishio, H.K.	Professor Emeritus
O'Toole, R.	Professor
Peressini, T.	Assistant Professor
Reitz, J.G.	Professor
Roman, R.	Associate Professor
Salaff, J.W.	Professor
Sev'er, A.	Associate Professor
Silva, E.	Professor
Simpson, J.H.	Professor
Sorenson, A.M.	Associate Professor
Spencer, M.W.	Professor Emeritus
Stein, A.	Associate Professor
Tanner, J.	Professor
Tepperman, L.	Professor, Chair
Ungar, S.	Associate Professor
Vanderburg, W.H.	Associate Professor
Veugelers, J.W.P.	Assistant Professor
Wellman, B.	Professor
Welsh, S.	Assistant Professor
Wheaton, B.	Professor
Zakuta, L.	Professor Emeritus
Zeitlin, I.M.	Professor Emeritus

2001-2002

Badgley, R.F.	Professor
Baldus, B.	Professor
Behrens, D.	Assistant Professor
Bernard, R.B.	Assistant Professor
Blute, M.	Associate Professor
Bodemann, Y.M.	Professor
Breton, R.	Professor Emeritus
Brownfield, D.	Associate Professor
Bryant, J.	Assistant Professor
Brym, R.	Professor
Campbell, D.F.	Professor Emeritus
Clark, S.D.	Professor Emeritus
Erickson, B.	Professor
Fong, W.C.	Associate Professor
Fox, B.	Associate Professor
Friedmann, H.	Professor
Gartner, R.	Professor
Giffen, P.J.	Professor Emeritus
Gillis, A.R.	Professor
Green, B.S.	Senior Lecturer
Hagan, J.	Professor
Hall, O.	Professor Emeritus
Hammond, M.	Associate Professor
Hannah-Moffat, K.	Assistant Professor
Hannigan, J.	Professor, Associate Chair
Harvey, E.B.	Professor
Howell, N.L.	Professor, Associate Chair
Hsiung, P.C.	Associate Professor
Isajiw, W.W.	Professor Emeritus
James, R.L.	Professor Emeritus
Jones, C.L.	Professor
Kalbach, W.	Professor Emeritus
Kelner, M.J.	Professor Emeritus
Kervin, J.B.	Professor
MacKay, R.W.	Associate Professor
Magee, W.J.	Assistant Professor

Magill, D.W.	Professor
Makler, H.M.	Professor Emeritus
Michelson, W.M.	Professor
Nishio, H.K.	Professor Emeritus
O'Toole, R.	Professor
Reitz, J.G.	Professor
Roman, R.	Associate Professor
Salaff, J.W.	Professor
Sev'er, A.	Associate Professor
Silva, E.	Professor
Simpson, J.H.	Professor
Sorenson, A.M.	Associate Professor
Spencer, M.W.	Professor Emeritus
Stein, A.	Associate Professor
Tanner, J.	Professor
Tepperman, L.	Professor, Chair
Ungar, S.	Associate Professor
Vanderburg, W.H.	Associate Professor
Veugelers, J.W.P.	Assistant Professor
Wellman, B.	Professor
Welsh, S.	Assistant Professor
Wheaton, B.	Professor
Zakuta, L.	Professor Emeritus
Zeitlin, I.M.	Professor Emeritus

2002-2003

Abraham, S.	Assistant Professor
Armstrong, I.	Adjunct Professor
Badgley, R.F.	Professor
Baldus, B.	Professor
Baumann, S.	Assistant Professor
Behrens, D.	Assistant Professor
Bernard, R.B.	Assistant Professor
Berry, B.	Assistant Professor
Blute, M.	Associate Professor
Bodemann, Y.M.	Professor
Boyd, M.	Professor
Breton, R.	Professor Emeritus
Brownfield, D.	Associate Professor
Bryant, J.	Associate Professor
Brym, R.	Professor
Campbell, D.F.	Professor Emeritus
Clark, S.D.	Professor Emeritus
Erickson, B.	Professor
Fong, W.C.	Associate Professor
Fox, B.	Associate Professor
Friedmann, H.	Professor
Gartner, R.	Professor
Giffen, P.J.	Professor Emeritus
Gillis, A.R.	Professor
Green, B.S.	Senior Lecturer
Hagan, J.	Professor
Hall, O.	Professor Emeritus
Hammond, M.	Associate Professor
Hannah-Moffat, K.	Assistant Professor
Hannigan, J.	Professor
Harvey, E.B.	Professor
Hermer, J.	Assistant Professor
Howell, N.L.	Professor
Hsiung, P.C.	Associate Professor
Isajiw, W.W.	Professor Emeritus
Jones, C.L.	Professor, Associate Chair

Kalbach, W.	Professor Emeritus
Kelner, M.J.	Professor Emeritus
Kervin, J.B.	Professor
Landolt, P.	Assistant Professor
MacKay, R.W.	Associate Professor
Magee, W.J.	Assistant Professor
Magill, D.W.	Professor, Associate Chair
Makler, H.M.	Professor Emeritus
Michelson, W.M.	Professor
Myles, J.	Professor
O'Toole, R.	Professor
Peng, I.	Associate Professor
Reitz, J.G.	Professor
Roman, R.	Associate Professor
Salaff, J.W.	Professor
Sev'er, A.	Associate Professor
Silva, E.	Professor Emeritus
Simpson, J.H.	Professor Emeritus
Sorenson, A.M.	Associate Professor
Spencer, M.W.	Professor Emeritus
Tanner, J.	Professor
Taylor, J.	Assistant Professor
Tepperman, L.	Professor, Chair
Ungar, S.	Associate Professor
Vanderburg, W.H.	Associate Professor
Veugelers, J.W.P.	Associate Professor
Wellman, B.	Professor
Welsh, S.	Associate Professor
Wheaton, B.	Professor
Zakuta, L.	Professor Emeritus
Zeitlin, I.M.	Professor Emeritus
Zhang, W.	Assistant Professor

*Editor's Note: Some of this information was taken from *A Quarter-Century of Sociology at the University of Toronto.*

Ph.D. Dissertations: 1966-1967 to 2002-2003

	TITLE	SUPERVISOR
1966		
Robin, M.	*Radical Politics and Organized Labour in Canada*	Clark, S.D.
1967		
Carlton, R.	*Differential Educational Achievement in a Bilingual Community*	Clark, S.D.
1968		
Crysdale, S.	*Occupational and Social Mobility in Riverdale, A Blue-Collar Community*	Clark, S.D.
1969		
Fullan, M.	*Workers' Receptivity to Industrial Change in Different Technological Settings*	Lobser, J.
Kelner, M.	*The Elite Structure of Toronto Ethnic Composition and Patterns of Recruitment*	Clark, S.D.
Sidlofsky, S.	*Post-war Immigrants in the Changing Metropolis*	Burnet, J.
1970		
Turk, J.	*The Measurement of Intra-Familial Power*	Bell, N.W.
Weinzweig, P.	*Socialization and Subculture in Elite Education: A Study of a Canadian Boys' Private School*	Weinberg, I.
1971		
Anderson, G.	*The Channel Facilitators Model of Migration: A Model Tested Using Portuguese Blue-Collar Immigrants in Metropolitan Toronto*	Breton, R.

	TITLE	SUPERVISOR
Lodhi, A.	*Urbanization, Criminality and Collective Violence: A Study in Sociology*	Giffen, P.J.
Maidman, F.	*Family Openness and Patterns of Adolescent Social Engagement*	Bell, N.W.
Maxwell, T.	*The French Population of Metro Toronto: A Study of Ethnic Participation and Ethnic Identity*	Hall, O.
Nkremdirim, B.	*Change, Power and Conflict: A Sociological Study of Collective Violence*	Breton, R.
Wayne, J.	*Networks of Informal Participation in a Suburban Context*	Michelson, W.

1972

Grayson, P.	*Neighbourhood and Voting: The Social Basis of Conservative Support in Broadview*	Walker, K.
O'Toole, R.	*The Sociology of Political Sects: Four Sects in Toronto in 1968-69. Vols. 1 and 2*	Feuer, L.
Segall, A.	*Sociocultural Variation in Illness Behaviour: A Comparative Study of Hospitalized Anglo-Saxon Protestant and Jewish Female Patients*	Bell, N.W.
Shulman, N.	*Urban Social Networks: An Investigation of Personal Networks in an Urban Setting*	Michelson, W.
White, T.	*Power and Autonomy in Organizations*	Nishio, H.K.

1973

Coburn, D.	*Work and Society: The Social Correlates of Job Control and Job Complexity*	Badgley, R.

	TITLE	SUPERVISOR
Earle, R.	*The Professional Mental Patient*	Bell, N.W.
Fiaz, M.	*Inter-Industrial Propensity to Strike in France 1890-1930*	Nishio, H.K.
Murphy, R.	*The Interpenetration of Professionalism and Bureaucracy*	Breton, R.
Powell, A.	*Participation in Issues as a Measure of Integration into a Small Town*	Breton, R.
Veevers, J.	*Voluntary Childless Wives: An Exploratory Study*	Bell, N.W.

1974

Butler, P.	*Involvement in Work and Family Worlds: A Study of Work-Family Linkages in Single-Earner and Dual-Earner Families*	Bell, N.W.
Foote, R.	*A Case Study: The Social Consequences of Rapid Industrialization*	Lucas, R.
Lee, D.	*The Impact of Modernization and Environmental Impingements Upon Nationalism and Separatism: The Quebec Case*	Isajiw, W.W.
McKie, C.	*An Ontario Industrial Elite: The Senior Executive in Manufacturing Industry*	Felt, L.
Pepperdene, B.	*The Occupation of Nursing and Careers: A Study of the Careers of Diploma and Degree Nurses*	Hall, O.
Strilaeff, F.	*Turnover of Nurses in Hospitals: A Study of a Service Organization*	Badgley, R.

	TITLE	SUPERVISOR
1975		
Clavir, J.	*"Better Conquer Hearts than Citadels": A Study in the Sociology of Culture and Social Change in Viet Nam*	Zeitlin, I.M.
Erinosho, A.	*Socio-Psychiatric Attributes and Therapeutic Structures as Predictors of Post-Hospital Performance: A Study of Two Psychiatric Centres in Nigeria*	Bell, N.W.
Himmelfarb, A.	*Fat Man, Thin World: A Participant Observation Study of Weight Watchers*	Zakuta, L.
Kennedy, L.	*Residential Mobility as a Cyclical Process: The Evaluation of the Home Environment both Before and After the Move*	Michelson, W.
Klein, W.	*Judicial Recruitment in Manitoba, Ontario and Quebec, 1905-1970*	Giffen, P.J.
1976		
Brym, R.	*Strangers and Rebels: The Russian-Jewish Intelligentsia in Marxist Social Movements at the Turn of the Twentieth Century*	Zeitlin, I.M.
D'Arcy, K.	*Change and Consequence in a Mental Health System: Theoretical and Empirical Chapters in a Sociology of Mental Illness*	Badgley, R.
Djao, A.	*Social Control in a Colonial Society: A Case Study of Working Class Consciousness in Hong Kong*	Baldus, B.
Ehrentraut, A.	*Technology and the Japanese Worker*	Nishio, H.K.

	TITLE	SUPERVISOR
Fetterley, R.	*Owners and Trainers: Patterns of Establishing and Maintaining Autonomy in a Worker-Client Relationship*	Hall, O.
Gerber, L.	*Minority Survival: Community Characteristics and Out-Migration from Indian Communities Across Canada*	Breton, R.
Glickman, Y.	*Organizational Indicators and Social Correlates of Collective Jewish Identity. Vols. 1 and 2*	Breton, R.
Konzak, B.	*Retirement and Aging in Canadian Society*	Nishio, H.K.
Makabe, T.	*Ethnic Group Identity: Canadian-Born Japanese in Metropolitan Toronto*	Isajiw, W.W.
Newson, J.	*The Roman-Catholic Clerical Exodus: A Study of Role Adaptation and Organizational Change*	Breton, R.
Plange, A.	*The Colonial State and Underdevelopment*	Wayne, J.
Reed, P.	*Life Style as an Element of Social Logic: Patterns of Activity, Social Characteristics, and Residential Choice*	Michelson, W.
Sacouman, J.	*Social Origins of Antigonish Movement Cooperative Associations in Eastern Nova Scotia*	Magill, D.W.
Trenton, T.	*Canadian Identity and Nationalism Among University Students: An Exploratory Analysis of the Applicability of Current Theory on Student Protest*	Walker, K.

	TITLE	SUPERVISOR
1977		
Adam, B.	*Social Psychology of Inferiorized People*	Baldus, B.
Blute, M.	*Darwinian Analogues and the Naturalistic Explanation of Purpose in Biology, Psychology, and the Sociocultural Sciences*	Isajiw, W.W.
Boudreau-Lemieux, F.	*Changes in the System for the Distribution of Psychiatric Care in Quebec, 1960-1974*	Bell, N.W.
Carveth, D.	*Sociologism and Psychoanalysis: A Study of Implicit Theories of Human Nature in "Symbolic Interactionism," "Reality Constructionism" and Psychoanalysis*	Zakuta, L.
Christy, R.	*Social Change and Post-Modernity: An Analysis of Social Space and Social Time in Canada and the United States*	Michelson, W.
Cohen, R.	*The Impact of Work-Setting on Clinical Training of Medical Students*	New, P.K.
Connidis, I.	*A Theoretical Development of Social Systems Analysis and an Examination of its Applicability to the Criminal Justice System*	Giffen, P.J.
Derow, E.	*Married Women's Employment and Domestic Labour*	Michelson, W.
Hammond, M.	*The Rise of the Pre-sapiens Theory in British and French Paleontology: A Study in the Sociology of Scientific Ideas*	Isajiw, W.W.
Lundy, K.	*The Effect of Organizational Setting on Secretary-Executive Interaction*	New, P.K.

	TITLE	SUPERVISOR
Martens, H.	*The Relationship of Religious to Socio-Economic Divisions among the Mennonites of Dutch-Prussian-Russian Descent in Canada*	Clark, S.D.
Petrunik, M.	*The Quest for Fluency: A Study of the Identity Problems and Management Strategies of Adult Stutterers and Some Suggestions for an Approach to the Management of Deviance*	Zakuta, L.
Schwartz, R.	*Utopia and Critical Theory*	Zeitlin, I.M.
Shearing, C.	*Real Men, Wise Men, Good Men and Cautious Men: A Study of Culture, Role Models and Interaction within a Police Communications Centre*	Zakuta, L.
Snider, L.	*Does the Legal System Reflect the Power Structure: A Test of Conflict Theory*	Turk, J.
Subramaniam, I.	*Identity-Shift: Post-Migration Changes in Identity among First-Generation East Indian Immigrants in Toronto*	Isajiw, W.W.
Wilson, S.	*The Changing Image of Canadian Women as Reflected in Popular Magazines, 1931-1970*	Tepperman, L.

1978

Brannigan, A.	*A Study of the Social Organization Discoveries in Science*	Turk, J.
Cape, E.	*"Going Downhill": Responses to Terminality in a Population of Institutionalized Aged Ill*	James, R.L.

	TITLE	SUPERVISOR
Craven, P.	*"An Impartial Umpire": Industrial Relations and the Canadian State, 1900-1911*	Baldus, B.
Effrat, M.	*Social Order and Unsocialized Behaviour: A Sociological Study of Privacy*	Isajiw, W.W.
Gilmore, A.	*Crowding: An Anatomy of a Spurious Paradigm*	Michelson, W.
Harris, M.	*Social Order and Individualized Behaviour: A Sociological Study of Privacy*	Isajiw, W.W.
Parakulam, G.	*Physical Density, Perceived Crowding and Reproductive Orientation*	Kalbach, W.
Runge, J.	*Progressive Educational Reform in Comparative Perspective*	Marsden, L.R.
Russell, S.	*Sex Role Socialization in the High School: A Study of the Perpetuation of Patriarchal Culture*	Breton, R.
Torrance, G.	*The Underside of the Hospital: Recruitment and the Meaning of Work among Non-Professional Hospital Workers*	New, P.K.
1979		
Bakker, H.	*Patrimonialism and Imperialism as Factors in Underdevelopment: A Comparative Historical Sociological Analysis of Java with Emphasis on Aspects of the Cultivation System, 1830-1870*	Zeitlin, I.M.

	TITLE	SUPERVISOR
Currie, A.	*Intra-Ethnic Marriage and Identification among German and Ukrainian Ethnic Groups in Canada: A Study of the Effect of Socioeconomic Status on Structural Ethnic Identification*	Kalbach, W.
Deutschmann, L.	*Decline of the WASP?: Dominant Group Identity in a Multi-ethnic Society*	Isajiw, W.W.
Gibbons, J.	*Artists, Dealers and Hustlers: The Art of Business or the Business of Art*	Badgley, R.
Giffin, K.	*Opportunities and Ideologies: Women in High-Status Professions in Bahia, Brazil*	Baldus, B.
Huxley, C.	*The Institutionalization of Industrial Conflict: A Comparative Analysis of Strike Activity in Britain and Canada since 1945*	Magill, D.W.
Lowe, G.	*The Administrative Revolution: The Growth of Clerical Occupations and the Development of the Modern Office in Canada, 1911-1931*	Magill, D.W.
Murray, S.	*Social Science Networks*	Magill, D.W.
Rhyne, D.	*Organizational Life in River City: A Case Study of Class, Ethnicity, Geographical Mobility and Status*	Turk, J.
Trottier, C.	*Teachers as Agents of Political Socialization*	Breton, R.

1980

Curtis, B.	*The Political Economy of Elementary Educational Development: Comparative Perspectives on State Schooling in Upper Canada*	Wayne, J.

	TITLE	SUPERVISOR
Donaldson, B.	*Cultural Legitimacy in the Australian Art World: A Study in the Sociology of Cultural Production*	Zakuta, L.
Farrelly, R.	*The Large Landowners of England and Wales, 1870-1939: An Elite in Transition*	O'Toole, R.
Giesbrecht, N.	*Changes in the Drinking Patterns of Skid Row Alcoholics: A Study in the Sociology of the Normalization of Deviants. Vols. 1 and 2*	Giffen, P.J.
MacLeod, H.	*The Transformation of the United Church of Canada, 1946-1977: A Study in the Sociology of the Denomination*	O'Toole, R.
McKendy, J.	*Max Weber and the Sociology of Roman Catholicism*	Zeitlin, I.M.
Milner, C.	*God, Saints, and Spirits: A Comparative Analysis of Brazilian Urban Medical Systems*	New, P.K.
Riggins, S.	*Institutional Change in Nineteenth-Century French Music*	Magill, D.W.
Sarginson, G.	*Explanation, Description and Historical Phenomena: A Critique of Organismic and Atomistic Theoretical Models in the Social Sciences*	Erickson, B.
Siddique, J.	*Work and Family in Contemporary Industrial Society: An Analysis of Canadian Data*	Turk, J.
Smith, R.D.	*Social Class and Health Behaviour. Vols. 1 and 2*	Badgley, R.
Van Vliet, W.	*Use, Evaluation and Knowledge of City and Suburban Environments by Children of Employed and Non-Employed Mothers*	Michelson, W.

	TITLE	SUPERVISOR
1981		
Allahar, A.	*Ideology and Practice: The Responses of the Cuban Sugar Planters to the Political and Economic Challenges of the 19th Century*	Murmis, M.
Carrington, P.	*Horizontal Co-optation Through Comparative Interlocks*	Tepperman, L.
Edgington, B.	*The Formation of the Asylum in Upper Canada*	Bell, N.W.
Laxer, G.	*The Social Origins of Canada's Branch-Plant Economy 1837-1914. Vols. 1 and 2*	Magill, D.W.
Listiak, A.	*Corporate Power and the Market: Automotive Performance and the Automobile Industry. Vols. 1 and 2*	Turk, J.
Meier, P.	*The Peasant Craftsmen of Otavalo, Ecuador*	Murmis, M.
Pilotta, J.	*Lived Nature and Self-Production: A Phenomenology of the Sensuous Universal*	Mackay, R.
Storey, R.	*Workers, Unions and Steel: The Shaping of the Hamilton Working Class, 1935-1948*	Turk, J.
Winson, A.	*Estate Agriculture, Capitalist Development and the State: The Specificity of Contemporary Costa Rica*	Murmis, M.
1982		
Anderson, K.	*Huron Women and Huron Men: The Effects of Demography, Kinship and the Social Division of Labour on Male/Female Relations among the 17th Century Huron*	Wayne, J.

Ph.D. Dissertations: 1966-1967 to 2002-2003

	TITLE	SUPERVISOR
Baker, R.	*Collaboration and Conflict: Scientific Change and the Structure of Biomedical Research*	Marsden, L.R.
Cheung, Y.	*The Social Organization of Missionary Medicine: A Study of Two Canadian Protestant Missions in China Before 1937*	New, P.K.
Corman, J.	*The Impact of State Ownership on a State Proprietary Corporation: The Potash Corporation of Saskatchewan*	Wellman, B.
Dasko, D.	*Incomes, Income Attainment and Income Inequality among Race-Sex Groups: A Test of the Dual Industry Theory*	Reitz, J.
Dickinson, J.	*Regulating the Uncertainties of Industrial Life: A Comparative Analysis of the Origins of Social Insurance in Britain and Germany, 1870-1914. Vols. 1 and 2*	Wayne, J.
Knutilla, M.	*The Impact of the Western Canadian Agrarian Movement on Federal Government Policy, 1900-1930: An Assessment and Analysis*	Brym, R.
Mann, S.	*Obstacles to Capitalist Development of Agriculture: An Analysis of the Class Structure and Uneven Development of Capitalist Agriculture, 1870-1930*	Wayne, J.
McAllister, H.	*Labour and the State: The Canadian Labour Congress, Consultative Forums, and Incomes Policies, 1960-1978*	Turk, J.
McDermott, P.	*Computers and Multinational Corporate Management Strategies*	Baldus, B.

	TITLE	SUPERVISOR
Morgan, C.	*Therapeutic Solutions to Deviance: The Social Organization of Treating Disturbed Young People*	Mackay, R.
Mostacci-Calzavara, L.	*Social Networks and Access to Job Opportunity*	Reitz, J.
Stasiulis, D.	*Race, Ethnicity and the State: The Political Structuring of South Asian and West Indian Communal Action in Combatting Racism*	Breton, R.

1983

Ghorayshi, P.	*Agricultural Development in Quebec: An Analysis of Production Units in the Agrarian Class Structure*	Zeitlin, I.M.
Minai, K.	*Continuity and Modernization in Postwar Japan: A Comparative Analysis of Farmers and Urban Employees*	Nishio, H.K.
O'Hearn, M.	*The Political Transformation of a Religious Order*	Magill, D.W.
Schenk, C.	*Massey Workers and Wage Controls: A Case Study of Mobilization and Coercive Integration*	Roman, R.
Tippin, D.	*The Legitimation of Social Change: Ontario Railways and the Idea of Progress, 1841-1884*	Baldus, B.

1984

Dajani, S.	*Health Care and Development: A Case Study of the Israeli-Occupied West Bank. Vols. 1 and 2*	Badgley, R.
Gannagé, C.	*Dividing Women and Men: The Role of the Company, the Union and the Family in a Canadian Garment Factory*	Turk, J.

	TITLE	SUPERVISOR
Jensen, P.	*Collective Bargaining of Nurses in Canada. Vols. 1, 2 and 3*	Badgley, R.
Richardson, J.	*A "Structural Rational" Theory of Financial-Nonfinancial Directorship Interlocks*	Tepperman, L.
Walters, R.	*Colonial Administrative Structures and Socio-Economic Development in the Island of Trinidad, 1498-1783*	Zeitlin, I.M.

1985

Boritch, H.	*The Making of Toronto the Good: The Organization of Policing and Production of Arrests, 1859-1955*	Hagan, J.
Gross, P.	*Kinship Structures in Remarriage Families*	Eichler, M.
Helmes-Hayes, R.	*Images of Inequality in Early Canadian Sociology 1922-1965. Vols. 1 and 2*	Baldus, B.
Ityavyar, D.	*The Development of Health Services in Nigeria, 1960-1985*	Wayne, J.
Menzies, R.	*Doing Violence: Psychiatric Discretion and the Prediction of Dangerousness. Vols. 1 and 2*	Ericson, R.
Reiter, E.	*Out of the Frying Pan and Into the Fryer: The Organization of Work in a Fast Food Outlet*	Turk, J.

1986

Beamish, R.	*A Study of Marx's Intellectual Labour Process: The Case of the Division of Labour*	Murmis, M.
Benjamin, M.	*The Organization of the Child Protective Service System in Metropolitan Toronto, 1978-1981: The Negotiation of Disorder*	Bell, N.W.

	TITLE	SUPERVISOR
Chunn, D.	*From Punishment to Doing Good: The Origins and Impact of Family Courts in Ontario, 1888-1942*	Ericson, R.
Hiscott, R.	*Transcending the Marginal Work World: A Sociological Analysis of Migration between Atlantic Canada and Ontario*	Magill, D.W.
Leighton, B.	*Examining Personal Network Communities*	Wellman, B.
Murphy, C.	*The Social and Formal Organization of Small Town Policing: A Comparative Analysis of R.C.M.P. and Municipal Policing*	Ericson, R.
Nauratil, Jr., K.	*Labor, Patronage and Social Structure in the Making of Medieval Architecture: France and England, 1000-1300*	Zeitlin, I.M.
O'Connor, J.	*Public Welfare Expenditure and Policy Orientation in O.E.C.D. Countries, 1960-1980*	Brym, R.
Owomero, B.	*Crime Trends and Patterns of Three African Countries, 1960-1979*	Turk, J.
Vaitkus, S.	*Intersubjectivity and the Social Group: An Investigation into Intersubjectivity as a Problem of the Social Group Based upon the Works of George Herbert Mead, Aron Gurwitsch and Alfred Schutz*	Mackay, R.
Visano, L.	*Staging a Deviant Career: The Social Organization of Male Street Prostitution*	Magill, D.W.
Wilson, M.	*Mexico's Oil Workers: Incorporation and Insurgency*	Roman, R.

	TITLE	SUPERVISOR
1987		
Asbury, K.	*Embedded Social Control: A Study of the Role of the Apartment Superintendent*	Giffen, P.J.
Bryant, J.	*Moral Codes and Social Structure in Ancient Greece: A Study on the Social Origins of Greek Ethics from Homer to the Epicureans and Stoics. Vols. 1 and 2*	Zeitlin, I.M.
Hanson, B.	*Attempts to Model Context: Senile Dementia in the Family as a Case Demonstration*	Bell, N.W.
Malarkey, R.	*The Emergence of Equal Pay Legislation in Ontario*	Hagan, J.
Martin, M.	*Communication and Social Forms: A Study of the Development of the Telephone System, 1876-1920*	Wayne, J.
1988		
Benoit, C.	*Midwives in Passage: A Case Study of Occupational Change*	Brym, R.
Jackson, L.	*In Whose Interests? A Study of Canadian Bilateral Aid to Jamaica's Agricultural Sector*	Murmis, M.
1989		
Abdo-Zubi, N.	*Colonial Capitalism and Rural Class Formation: An Analysis of the Processes of Social Economic and Political Change in Palestine, 1920-1947*	Wayne, J.
Chan, H.M.	*Rethinking Ideology and Organization in China*	Nishio, H.K.

	TITLE	SUPERVISOR
Keane, C.R.	*Loose Coupling in Tight Places: Gender and Psychological Strain among Public Housing Residents*	Gillis, R.
Koc, M.	*Persistence Despite Differentiation: Tobacco Producers of Aegean Turkey*	Friedmann, H.
Lenton, R.	*The Disciplining of Children in the Home: An Empirical Assessment*	Eichler, M.
MacMahon, M.W.	*Trends in Corrections in Ontario*	Ericson, R.
Neis, B.	*The Organization of Workers in the Newfoundland Fishery, 1920-1970*	Turk, J.
Smandych, R.C.	*Asylums, Prisons and Poorhouses: The Upper Canada Experience with Institutional Reform, 1830-1950*	Ericson, R.

1990

Hall, A.	*Production Politics and the Construction of Consent: A Case Study of Health and Safety in Mining*	Wayne, J.
Koc, S.	*Peasants' Hegemon and the Politics of "Normal Times": The Cases of the Republican People's Party and the Democrat Party, Turkey*	Bodemann, M.
Lank, H.	*Sojourning: The Process of Adaptation of Canadians in Geneva, Switzerland*	Isajiw, W.W.
McCarthy, W.	*Life on the Street: Serious Theft, Drug-Selling and Prostitution among Homeless Youth*	Hagan, J.
Moore, G.	*The Information Industry in Ontario: A Test of the Post-Industrial Thesis*	Marsden, L.R.
Olsen, G.	*On the Limits of Social Democracy: The Rise and Fall of the Swedish Wage Earner Funds*	Brym, R.

	TITLE	SUPERVISOR
1991		
Arnold, B.	*A Life Course Dynamics Approach to Professional Deviance and Self-Regulation: The Case of Ontario Lawyers*	Hagan, J.
Biezenski, R.	*The Role of the Intelligentsia in the Polish Trade Union NSZZ "Solidarnosc"*	Wayne, J.
Henriques, H.	*Hidden from History: Structures of Internal Dependency and Indigenous Class Formation in British Guiana, 1808-1856*	Wayne, J.
Kellough, G.	*The Abortion Controversy: A Study of Law, Culture and Social Change*	Ericson, R.
Kelly, K.	*Non-Capitalist Relations and Agricultural Production: Reinterpretation of the Economic History of 19th Century Lower Canada*	Friedmann, H.
Nelson, R.	*The Reception and Development of the Sociology of Knowledge in American Sociology, 1936-1960*	Zeitlin, I.M.
1992		
Ajzner, J.	*Modern Community, Virtue, and Conflict: The American Intellectual Elite and the Vietnam War*	Simpson, J.
Bell, S.	*Controlling Delinquents: An Analysis of the Role of the Family in the Young Offender Court*	Hagan, J.
Espinoza, V.	*Networks of Informal Economy: Work and Community Among Santiago's Urban Poor*	Wellman, B.
Kay, F.	*A Profession in Transition: Gender and Career Mobility in Law*	Hagan, J.

	TITLE	SUPERVISOR
LaCombe, D.	*Power, Knowledge, and Law: The Politics of Pornography Law Reform*	Ericson, R.
Mosher, C.	*The Legal Response to Narcotic Drugs in Five Ontario Cities*	Hagan, J.
Sugiman, P.	*Labour's Dilemma: The Meaning and Politics of Worker Resistance in a Gendered Setting*	Marsden, L.R.

1993

Baber, Z.	*Science, Technology and Colonial Power in India: A Study in the Historical Sociology of Science*	Zeitlin, I.M.
Davies, S.	*In Search of the Culture Clash: Evaluating a Sociological Theory of Social Class Inequality in Education*	Tanner, J.
Grimes, R.E.	*Race, Rape, and the Death Penalty Revisited*	Hagan, J.
Lee, W.	*Industrial and Labour Market Segmentation in Singapore*	Reitz, J.
O'Grady, W.	*Coming of Age on the Periphery: Youth Unemployment and the Transition to Adulthood in Newfoundland*	Tanner, J.
Tyyska, V.	*The Women's Movement and the Welfare State: Child Care Policy in Canada and Finland 1960-1990*	Marsden, L.R.

1994

Denis, C.	*False Hopes: The New Democratic Party of Canada in Quebec in the 1988 Federal Election*	Brym, R.
LeNavenec, C.L.	*The Illness Career of Family Subsystems Experiencing Dementia: Predominant Phases and Styles of Managing*	Bell, N.W.

	TITLE	SUPERVISOR
Lewis, J.	*Identify Transformation: The Experience of HIV-positive Gay Men*	Lee, J.
Podolsky, M.	*Kaigai-Shijo Socialization: A Study of Children of Japanese Temporary Residents in Toronto, Canada*	Isajiw, W.W.
Roxborough, S.	*Women, Work and Well-being: A Consideration of Workplace and Home Contingencies*	Turner, J.
Ruemper, W.	*Formal and Informal Social Control of Incarcerated Women in Ontario, 1857-1931*	Gartner, R.
Tindall, D.B.	*Collective Identity and Participation in the Vancouver Island Wilderness Preservation Movement*	Erickson, B.
Uneke, O.	*Intergroup Differences in Self-employment: Blacks and Chinese in Toronto*	Reitz, J.

1995

Kassam, M.	*The Birth of the Work Ethos in Ontario 1885-1910: The Social Construction of Attitudes Towards Work and the Working People*	Baldus, B.
Kim, A.	*A Protestant Christianity in South Korea: A Historical Cultural Reception and Social Impact, 1910-1989*	Zeitlin, I.M.
Klassen, T.	*The Process of Organizational Decline and Death: Internal and External Factors Precipitating the Decline of the Ontario Ministry of Skills Development 1985-1993*	Reitz, J.
LeBlanc, S.	*The Influence of Structural Factors on the Early Retirement Plans and Expectations of Older Workers*	Marshall, V.

	TITLE	SUPERVISOR
Mann, R.	*The Politics and Experience of Domestic Abuse*	Gartner, R.
Manuel, L.	*Constructing the Dementia Process: The Identification and Management of Alzheimer's Disease*	Salaff, J.
McMullin, J.	*Connecting Age, Gender, Class and Ethnicity: A Case Study of the Garment Industry in Montreal*	Marshall, V.
Okolie, A.	*Oil Revenues, International Credits and Food Policies in Nigeria, 1970-1992*	Friedmann, H.
Roszell, T.	*A Life Course Perspective on the Implications of Stress*	Wheaton, B.
Suyyagh, F.	*Ethnic Enterprise and the Community Dimension: The Case of Arab Business Leaders in Toronto, Ontario, Canada*	Isajiw, W.W.
Theriault, L.	*The Location of Pharmaceutical R & D in Canada: An Examination of the Managerial Perception in 1993*	Magill, D.W.
Winston, N.	*Experiencing the System: A Sociological Analysis of Identification in the European Union*	Breton, R.
Wortley, S.	*Social Networks, Social Support, and Substance Abuse*	Wellman, B.

1996

Adams, T.	*A Dentist & a Gentleman: The Significance of Gender to the Establishment of the Dental Profession*	Fox, B.
Chung, J.	*Development, Work and Family in the Making of Korean Working Women*	Fox, B.

	TITLE	SUPERVISOR
Singh, S.	*Construction of an Indian Ethno-Religious Identity within the Context of Ethnic Diversity: A Case Study of a Hindu Temple in Toronto*	Bodemann, M.
Smaller, E.	*A Simple & Unsophisticated Life: Rural Development Policy in the Face of Social and Economic Volatility: Himachal Pradesh, India*	Wayne, J.
Smith, T.	*Psychosocial Determinants of Perceived Social Support among Former Psychiatric Patients*	Turner, J.
Xia, G.	*Confucianisam & Its Model Relevance: A Dialogue with the West*	Zeitlin, I.M.
Zawilski, V.	*Saving Russia: Russian Nationalism in Transition 1965-1995*	Breton, R.

1997

Atasoy, Y.	*Beyond Tradition and Resistance: Islamic Politics and Global Relations of Power: The Case of Turkey 1839-1990*	Friedmann, H.
Marino, F.	*Social Class and Fear of Crime: A Descriptive Analysis and Test of Social Vulnerability as an Explanation of Class Differences in Crime Fear*	Turner, J.
Obosu-Mensah, K.	*Food Production in Urban Areas: A Case Study of Urban Agriculture in Accra, Ghana*	Michelson, W.
Yang, B.	*Personal Values and Electronic Media Adoption and Post-Adoption in Urban China*	Silva, E.

	TITLE	SUPERVISOR
1998		
Amor, M.	*State Persecution and Vulnerability: A Comparative Historical Analysis of Violent Ethnocentrism*	Zeitlin, I.M.
Gobin, D.	*The Differential Incorporation of Racial Minority Youths: Indo-Caribbean, Afro-Caribbean and Punjabi Sikh Teens in Toronto and Surrounding Areas*	Isajiw, W.W.
Hall, K.	*Gender, Marital Status and Psychiatric Disorder: An Examination of Social Causation vs. Social Selection Explanations for the Gender Specific Benefits of Marriage for Mental Health*	Wheaton, B.
Macmillan, R.	*Growing Up Scared: The Effects of Violent Victimization in Adolescence on Adult Socio-economic Attainment*	Hagan, J.
Mookodi, G.	*"We are Struggling" Gender, Poverty and the Dynamics of Survival Within Low Income Households in Botswana*	Howell, N.
Potter, S.	*The Social Resources of Immigrants: Effects on the Integration of Independent and Family Class Immigrants to Toronto, Canada from South Asia*	Reitz, J.
Puri, D.	*Gift of a Daughter: Change and Continuity in Marriage Patterns among Two Generations of North Indians in Toronto and Delhi*	Howell, N.
1999		
Llovet, I.	*New Social Relations in Argentinean Agriculture: Capitalist Sharecropping in the Pampean Region*	Roman, R.

	TITLE	SUPERVISOR
Lloyd, D.	*Socioeconomic Consequences of Early-Onset Psychiatric Disorders: Mental Illness and Stress in a Life Course Perspective*	Erickson, B.
Torok, P.	*Hungarian Church-State Relationships: A Socio-historical Analysis*	O'Toole, R.
Verma, N.	*Arrival, Survival and Beyond Survival: Indo-Trinidadian Quest for Political and Cultural Ascendency*	Bodemann, M.
2000		
Butovsky, J.	*Decline of the New Democratic Party: The Politics of Postmaterialism or Neo Liberalism*	Brym, R.
Butters, J.	*Understanding Adolescent Cannabis Use: A Stress Process Application*	Erickson, P.
Dawson, M.	*Intimacy and Justice: The Role of Victim-Defendant Relationship in Criminal Justice Decision-making*	Gartner, R.
Dimitrova, D.	*The Telework Mosaic, How People Telework*	Salaff, J.
Dinovitzer, R.	*Moving Up or Moving Out: Social Capital and Migration in Lawyers' Lives*	Hagan, J.
Foster, H.	*Neighbourhood and Family Contexts of Gendered Aggression in Childhood*	Hagan, J.
Kaukinen, C.	*The Help-Seeking of Violent Crime Victims*	Gartner, R.
Mushkat, D.	*Rethinking Jewish Vitality: Exploring Sources of Significance, Affection and Change in Traditional Jewish Ritual Observance*	Isajiw, W.W.

	TITLE	SUPERVISOR
Nazer, N.	*Operating Virtually Within a Hierarchical Framework: How a Virtual Organization Really Works*	Wellman, B.
Nierobisz, A.	*In the Shadow of the Economy: Judicial Decisions on Wrongful Dismissal in Eras of Economic Uncertainty*	Gartner, R., Welsh, S.
Regoeczi, W.	*Re-examining the Density Debate: A New Slant on an Ongoing Problem*	Gillis, R.
2001		
Bastani, S.	*Middle Class Community in Tehran: Social Networks, Social Support and Marital Relationships*	Wellman, B.
Hampton, K.	*Living the Wired Life in the Wired Suburb: Netville, Globalization and Civic Society*	Wellman, B.
Matheson, F.	*Hostile Women, Sullen Men and the Social-Psychological Consequences of Power, Control and the Occupational Personality*	Gillis, R.
Ooka, E.	*Growing Up Canadian: Language, Culture and Identity among Second-Generation Chinese Youths in Canada*	Fong, E.
Raddon, M.	*Toward a New Harmony of Money and Reciprocity: Community Currencies in a Gendered Economy*	Friedmann, H.
Wilkes, R.	*Competition or Colonialism? A Comparison of Two Theories of Ethnic Collective Action, 1981-2000*	Fong, E.
2002		
Albanese, P.	*Mothers of the Nation, Guardians of the Hearth: Women, Family and Nationalism in 20th-Century Europe*	Eichler, M.

Ph.D. Dissertations: 1966-1967 to 2002-2003

	TITLE	SUPERVISOR
Asbridge, M.	*Classifying Lifestyles: A Re-examination of the Drug-Crime Nexus among Toronto High School Youth*	Tanner, J.
Eid, P.	*Ethnic and Religious Identity Retention among Second-Generation Arab Youths in Montreal*	Isajiw, W.W.
Karakayali, N.	*Simmel's Stranger: In Theory and In Practice*	Zeitlin, I.M.
Wolfe, K.	*Reciprocity of Intergenerational Mental Health Problems: A Study of the Effects of Children's Age, Sex and Family Structure*	Howell, N.

Appendices

Appendix A
List of Teaching Staff by Year Prior to 1963-1964*

1934-1935

Hart, C.W.M. Lecturer in Anthropology
Ketchum, J.D. Assistant Professor of Psychology
Urwick, E.J. Professor of Economics

1935-1936

Hart, C.W.M. Lecturer in Anthropology and Supervisor of Studies in Sociology
Ketchum, J.D. Assistant Professor of Psychology
Urwick, E.J. Professor of Economics

1936-1937

Clark, S.D. Instructor
Hart, C.W.M. Assistant Professor of Anthropology and Supervisor of Studies in Sociology
Ketchum, J.D. Assistant Professor of Psychology
Urwick, E.J. Professor of Economics

1937-1938

Franz, J.G. Instructor in Sociology
Hart, C.W.M. Assistant Professor of Anthropology and Supervisor of Studies in Sociology
Ketchum, J.D. Assistant Professor of Psychology
Urwick, E.J. Professor Emeritus

1938-1939

Clark, S.D. Lecturer in Sociology
Hart, C.W.M. Assistant Professor of Anthropology and Supervisor of Studies in Sociology
Ketchum, J.D. Assistant Professor of Psychology
Urwick, E.J. Professor Emeritus

1939-1940

Clark, S.D. Lecturer in Sociology
Hart, C.W.M. Assistant Professor of Sociology
Ketchum, J.D. Assistant Professor of Psychology
Urwick, E.J. Professor Emeritus

1940-1941

Clark, S.D. Lecturer in Sociology
Devereux, E.G. Instructor in Sociology
Hart, C.W.M. Assistant Professor of Sociology
Ketchum, J.D. Assistant Professor of Psychology
Urwick, E.J. Professor Emeritus

1941-1942*

Clark, S.D. Lecturer
Devereux, E.G. Instructor
Hart, C.W.M. Assistant Professor
[Editor's Note: Beginning in 1941-1942 all appointments are in Sociology]

1942-1943

Clark, S.D. Lecturer
Hart, C.W.M. Assistant Professor
Ross, A.D. Instructor

1943-1944

Clark, S.D. Lecturer
Hart, C.W.M. Assistant Professor
Ross, A.D. Instructor
Younge, E.R. Instructor

1944-1945

Clark, S.D. Assistant Professor
Hart, C.W.M. Associate Professor
Marshall, D.G. Lecturer
Ross, A.D. Instructor

1945-1946

Burnet, J.R. Instructor
Clark, S.D. Assistant Professor

Giffen, P.J. Instructor
Hart, C.W.M. Associate Professor

1946-1947

Burnet, J.R. Instructor
Clark, S.D. Assistant Professor
Hart, C.W.M. Associate Professor
Lipset, S.M. Lecturer

1947-1948

Burnet, J.R. Lecturer
Chinoy, E. Lecturer
Clark, S.D. Assistant Professor
Hart, C.W.M. Associate Professor
Lipset, S.M. Lecturer
Wargon, S.T. Teaching Fellow

1948-1949

Chinoy, E. Lecturer
Clark, S.D. Associate Professor
Giffen, P.J. Lecturer
Wargon, S.T. Teaching Fellow
Watson, J.W. Instructor

1949-1950

Burnet, J.R. Lecturer
Chinoy, E. Lecturer
Clark, S.D. Associate Professor
Giffen, P.J. Lecturer
Pullman, D.R. Teaching Fellow

1950-1951

Burnet, J.R. Lecturer
Chinoy, E. Lecturer
Clark, S.D. Associate Professor
Giffen, P.J. Lecturer
Pullman, D.R. Instructor
Seeley, J.R. Associate Professor (part-time)
Sim, R.A. Assistant Professor (part-time)

1951-1952

Burnet, J.R. Lecturer
Clark, S.D. Associate Professor
Geiger, T. J. Professor (Visiting)
Giffen, P.J. Lecturer
Riemersma, J.C. Lecturer
Ryder, N.B. Lecturer
Seeley, J.R. Associate Professor (part-time)
Sim, R.A. Assistant Professor (part-time)

1952-1953

Burnet, J.R.Lecturer
Clark, S.D. Associate Professor
Riemersma, J.C. Lecturer
Ryder, N.B. Lecturer
Seeley, J.R. Associate Professor (part-time)
Sim, R.A. Assistant Professor (part-time)
Zakuta, L. Lecturer

1953-1954

Burnet, J.R. Lecturer
Clark, S.D. Professor
Giffen, P.J. Lecturer
Ryder, N.B. Lecturer
Seeley, J.R. Associate Professor (part-time)
Sim, R.A. Assistant Professor (part-time)
Zakuta, L. Lecturer

1954-1955

Burnet, J.R. Assistant Professor
Clark, S.D. Professor
Giffen, P.J. Lecturer
Watson, R.E.L. Instructor
Zakuta, L. Lecturer

1955-1956

Burnet, J.R. Assistant Professor
Clark, S.D. Professor
Giffen, P.J. Assistant Professor

Mann, W.E. Instructor
Wrong, D.H. Lecturer
Zakuta, L. Lecturer

1956-1957

Burnet, J.R. Assistant Professor
Clark, S.D. Professor
Giffen, P.J. Assistant Professor
Hall, O. Professor
Richter, M.N. Lecturer
Zakuta, L. Lecturer

1957-1958

Burnet, J.R. Assistant Professor
Clark, S.D. Professor
Giffen, P.J. Assistant Professor
Hall, O. Professor
Zakuta, L. Lecturer

1958-1959

Burnet, J.R. Assistant Professor
Clark, S.D. Professor
Giffen, P.J. Assistant Professor
Hall, O. Professor
Zakuta, L. Lecturer

1959-1960

Burnet, J.R. Assistant Professor
Clark, S.D. Professor
Giffen, P.J. Assistant Professor
Hall, O. Professor
Keyfitz, N. Professor
Zakuta, L. Assistant Professor

1960-1961

Burnet, J.R. Assistant Professor
Carr-Saunders, A. Professor (Visiting)
Clark, S.D. Professor
Giffen, P.J. Assistant Professor

Hall, O. Professor
Hill, D.G. Instructor
Keyfitz, N. Professor
McFarlane, B.A. Special Lecturer
Zakuta, L. Assistant Professor

1961-1962

Burnet, J.R. Assistant Professor
Clark, S.D. Professor
Giffen, P.J. Assistant Professor
Hall, O. Professor
Keyfitz, N. Professor
Nishio, H.K. Special Lecturer
Zakuta, L. Assistant Professor

1962-1963

Burnet, J.R. Assistant Professor
Clark, S.D. Professor
Coughlin, R.J. Special Lecturer
Giffen, P.J. Assistant Professor
Hall, O. Professor
Keyfitz, N. Professor
Lucas, R.A. Special Lecturer
Seals, R.C. Lecturer
Willmott, D.E. Instructor
Zakuta, L. Assistant Professor

* Editor's Note: The information in this appendix was taken from *A Quarter-Century of Sociology at the University of Toronto.*

Appendix B
Ph.D. Dissertations in Sociology Completed Prior to 1963*

YEAR	STUDENT	TOPIC
1925	Fisher, H.E.	*Professional Associations in Canada*
1926	Cheng, T.-F.	*Oriental Immigration in Canada*
1929	Cotton, L.E.	*The Principle of Group Activity*
1932	Hamilton, C.R.	*Education in the Life of the People: A Study of its Place in the Social Life of Modern England*
1937	Bryce, L.W.	*The Changing Family in India*
1953	Mann, W.E.	*Sect and Cult in Alberta*
1960	Hill, D.G.	*Negroes in Toronto: A Sociological Study of a Minority Group*
1960	Pullman, D.R.	*A Study of Social Organization in Relation to Economic Change*
1960	Watson, R.E.L.	*The Nova Scotia Teachers' Union: A Study in the Sociology of Formal Organizations*

* Editor's Note: The information in this appendix was taken from *A Quarter-Century of Sociology at the University of Toronto.*

Appendix C
Editor's Introduction to the 1988 publication
A Quarter-Century of Sociology at the University of Toronto

As its title may be a trifle deceiving, it should be noted at the outset that this little book does not provide a comprehensive, critical history of the University of Toronto Department of Sociology since 1963. That is not its purpose. Instead, it has been put together as a memento intended to celebrate the department's twenty-fifth anniversary.

Those with even a passing familiarity with the history of the department will know that, as in all departments of Sociology, there have been stormy and difficult times at Toronto. The conflicts between individuals and factions over issues normally referred to as "office" or "departmental polities" tend in departments such as Sociology to be rendered more Byzantine in their complexity and more difficult of resolution by the fact that sociology is an inherently "political" discipline in the broader sense of that term. Thus, at Toronto as elsewhere, matters of day-to-day administration become tangled in wider political disputes to a degree that they do not in other disciplines and departments in the university. Such matters, while worthy of sociological investigation, are not addressed in this volume and so readers looking for a muck-raking exposé—the inside story of what *really* happened between 1963 and 1988—will be disappointed by the contents of the book. In a volume written on short notice and intended to be commemorative, if not mildly celebratory, a detailed, critical history of the department seemed both impossible and inappropriate.

This does not mean that the book is barren of historical or sociological interest. It contains much that historians of sociology will find useful; year-by-year lists of teaching staff and Ph.D. dissertations completed as well as original essays about the department written by two of its distinguished, long-time members, S.D. Clark and Oswald Hall. Professor Simpson and I chose Professors Clark and Hall to contribute to the volume on the grounds that they alone among a number of eminent senior members of the department are Professors Emeriti of the University, Fellows of the Royal

Society of Canada, and Honorary Presidents of the Canadian Sociology and Anthropology Association. Students of the history of sociology and those with a more casual interest in the history of the department will alike find their essays to be absorbing reading. Professor Clark's essay, "How the Department of Sociology Came into Being," recounts the early (pre-1963) development of Sociology at the University of Toronto from the point of view of one who was an "insider" to the process. Professor Hall's contribution, "Some Recollections of Sociology in Two Universities: McGill and the University of Toronto," draws on his experience in the two departments to offer us—again from an insider's vantage point—a systematic comparison of selected aspects of the development of Sociology at McGill and the University of Toronto. Without reading too much into either of their essays, it is fair to say, I think, that they hint at some of the contentious issues that a careful scholarly analysis of the department's history would involve. Toronto has long been a major centre of academic sociology in Canada, and so a full-scale history of the department, while difficult, would certainly be an interesting and useful undertaking.

By way of closing, I would like to offer some points of information about the volume and to thank some of the people who were involved in its preparation. I gathered the information in Chapters 3 and 4 and Appendices A and B. I was assisted in various ways by different people in the preparation of this material, and I have acknowledged their help where appropriate. Any errors or omissions are my responsibility.

For their assistance during the course of the carrying out of this project I would like to offer special thanks to Professors John Simpson, S.D. Clark, and Oswald Hall. I am indebted to Professor Simpson on two counts. First, he was a helpful and encouraging "ghost editor." Second, by engaging me to oversee the production of this little book, he offered me the chance to interact with two of the makers of Canadian sociology. This allowed me the rare opportunity to experience a little of the history of the discipline as close to "first-hand" as is possible without actually having been there. For their part, Professors Hall and Clark made it a valuable learning experience. They were gracious and generous in their responses to my often-naive queries about the history of Canadian sociology and I would like to thank them for their patience and assistance.

As a final note, I want to thank Drs. Richard Schmidt and Gabrielle MacDonald of the Writing Lab at New College, University of Toronto, and Michael Parker of the Classics Department of Memorial University for "technical" editorial assistance.

R. Helmes-Hayes
August 1988

Appendix D
Chairman's Introduction to the 1988 publication *A Quarter-Century of Sociology at the University of Toronto*

This small volume commemorates the twenty-fifth anniversary of the establishment of the Department of Sociology in the University of Toronto. It is not, as the editor points out, a history of the Department of Sociology at Toronto. It does make available some facts and interpretations that should cause the work of writing a history of the department to be easier than would otherwise have been the case. Thus, this volume points to the future as much as it memorializes the past.

The volume had its origin in a meeting of Professors Dennis Magill and Lorna Marsden and myself in the fall of 1987 where the general contents were outlined. Given his interest in the history of sociology in Canada and his scholarly credentials, it was agreed that Dr. Rick Helmes-Hayes should be invited to serve as editor. Fortunately, he accepted our offer. His superb research and editorial skills have brought our ideas to fruition. By way of friendly comment on Dr. Helmes-Hayes' introduction to this volume I would note that in my experience not all departments of Sociology are politically feisty nor is sociology any more inherently political in the broad sense of that term than many other university disciplines.

Special thanks are due Professors Emeriti S.D. Clark and Oswald Hall for agreeing to write the essays appearing herein. They are rich sources of insight into the milieu that have influenced the department and into the dynamics of its collective life.

For those readers who are not members of the professional company of sociologists, this volume provides some insight into the nature of the sociological task and its implementation at Toronto.

For sociologists in Canada and elsewhere this volume provides some data that may prove useful for assessing the contribution of sociology at Toronto to the discipline so far.

John H. Simpson
September 1988

AGMV Marquis
MEMBER OF SCABRINI MEDIA
Quebec, Canada
2003